THE

SOURCE

ADVENTURE

Vywamus

Channeled by Janet McClure

Edited by Lillian Harben

OTHER BOOKS THROUGH JANET McCLURE

AHA!
The Realization Book

Collected Channelings
Volume 1 & 2

Du Hast Die Wahl
(You Have the Choice)

Light Techniques
That Trigger Transformation

Sanat Kumara
Training a Planetary Logos

Scopes of Dimensions:
How to Experience
Multi-Dimensional Reality

THE SOURCE ADVENTURE
Vywamus, Channeled by Janet McClure

Copyright ©1988 by the Tibetan Foundation

Published by Light Technology Publishing
P.O. Box 1526, Sedona, AZ 86339
(602) 282-6523

ISBN NO. 0-929385-06-03

Printed by Mission Possible Printing

INTRODUCTION TO VYWAMUS

My Friends,

I, Djwhal Khul, have the privilege of introducing to you Vywamus - a great Being who has come among us to serve during these critical, yet marvelous, times when humanity seeks to evolve into spiritual consciousness, casting off the outworn "forms" and moving in greater light into the New Age. Many spiritual teachers are appearing to help mankind and Mother Earth make this transition as painless and clear as possible and at as high a level as possible.

Vywamus, then, is One of a very elevated consciousness. Vywamus is an evolved aspect of Sanat Kumara (our Planetary Logos) who ensouls the earth and all upon it and within it. The Earth, in effect, is being "held together" by his focus of consciousness. At a still higher level of this consciousness is Vywamus. He can be equated to the "higher self," as we sometimes refer to it, or the soul of Sanat Kumara.

Vywamus evolved to his present "position" through the physical chain - just as humanity has chosen to do. Vywamus chose to express in physical existence aeons ago, and did this on a planet similar to Earth. While in physical existence he was offered the opportunity to be a channel for higher energies, and in thus serving gained clear perception and quickly passed on to the spiritual plane.

This was accomplished after only thirty-seven incarnations on the physical.

Now, in his great love, he has chosen to assist mankind. An exceptional channel, Janet McClure, brings through this teaching book which he offers to mankind with his love.

Gratefully accept these teachings, my friends, as I do.

DJWHAL KHUL

About the Author

Janet McClure is a dedicated, committed and loving being who channels many spiritual teachers with extraordinary clarity.

Her channeling career began after she had been studying intensively with the Brotherhood of the White Temple, from which correspondence college she received a Doctorate in Metaphysics, and dedicated herself to the service of the Cosmic Plan.

She had been working in business areas while studying metaphysics. Her life changed 180 degrees when she was approached by Djwhal Khul through her intuition and was asked to be a channel for him. Djwhal had been asked by Sanat Kumara (his teacher and the planetary Logos) to return to his earth contacts and aid humanity as he had done when he channeled the information to Alice Bailey 40 years earlier. Djwhal set about making a choice of who to come through and saw that Janet had extensive channeling experience in previous lives and had taught channeling in Egypt. He knew that channeling would come rather easily to her.

Upon being approached by Djwhal and offered this opportunity, Janet accepted immediately and enthusiastically. Her Aries nature allows her to move forward on the leading edge of new age awareness without fear of falling. Vywamus says that many are asked to serve but few respond due to not hearing or feeling that certain responsibilities in their lives have yet to be met.

Janet says of her own evolution, "The benefits to me of channeling in terms of clearing blocked areas and increasing light frequency have been enormous. My evolution is accelerated a great deal through the channeling process. That is one reason why Vywamus chose to train channels; because he believes it to be the single most important step you can take to forward your evolution."

TABLE OF CONTENTS

INTRODUCTION

Have you often asked yourself why you exist? Why you are here? What is the purpose of life? I give you this answer. You are discovering - you are processing - existence.

The process, then, is the means to discover, to learn, to grow, to recognize opportunities - to be aware. Awareness is the process.

Let me, in the following material, take you on a journey of awareness. It will be a means to explore deeply, sometimes conceptually, all of existence. For those of you who are just now asking the question, "Who am I?", allow this book to enlarge your concept of self beyond your present understanding. Your question is: " What is the purpose of life?" "What is the process for?" This material has been written especially for you. There is definitely a "stretching, or bridging," process that I will guide you through.

Before now, portions of this material have been available in booklet form. This book represents a collection of the material in a cohesive form, with the addition of several sections of new material. It answers many questions that previously seemed unanswerable

I refer to Source Light and Its evolution frequently in order to show you the means by which you may fit self into the whole picture. Try to allow this stretch. If it seems to you that the Source is beyond your present understanding, know that this is not true. You are a part of that Source and Its Light.

Come along with me on this exciting adventure and allow the process to work through you. It is not accidental that you have obtained this book. Seek to utilize it as a tool to increase your understanding. Whatever speaks to you in the book, allow it to do so. The material may speak in many ways, sometimes obvious, sometimes subtle, but recognize that this book is brought to you by your soul as an opportunity to learn and to grow in your understanding.

Love,

Vywamus

CHAPTER 1

EVOLUTION:
THE SEVEN LEVELS

Let us begin our exploration of the Source and Its evolution. We will be discussing specifics in this unfolding saga of how the Oneness develops or evolves. I give you a little "story" which is my understanding of the Source's beginning or a new opportunity as it may have occurred.

The Source was "thinking." Universal consciousness at its point of origination was seeking to resolve a specific point. Just as each of you may seek to understand an area of your life, the Source also seeks to understand. Perhaps It considered the following:

How will this particular situation look if I as the Source look at it from seven points of view at once?

The Source considered.
The Source reflected.
The Source synthesized.
The Source realized.
The Source decided.
The Source acted.

And thus a seven-point program was begun. The Source activated and sent forth parts of itself (Divine

Sparks or Evolving Consciousnesses) to a specific point that we will call level seven of the spiritual plane. This level was but a step for these parts of the Source. It was not far from the consciousness level of the Source Itself. Some of these sparks or beings could be referred to as those who have an encompassing ability to understand, to see a universal point of view. Now these sparks, these parts of the Source, Itself, maintained in a sense a pattern of themselves at this level, but their true essence began to stretch out more and more. It stretched and reached what we call the sixth level, left a pattern of self there, stretched and reached the fifth level, left a pattern of self there, and continued in this manner through the fourth, third, second and first levels of what we call the Spiritual plane. That was the beginning of the involution from the Source into denser and denser matter.

Now still eagerly did the Source seek to learn. To stretch forth now beyond this seven-fold division required a major division point because of the way that existence had been framed by the Source for this specific exploration, or, you could say, for the Source's intellectual exercise. Having explored seven, leaving an energy pattern of self, It became aware of a division point and the need to keep stretching forth.

At this particular point, the stretch became, one could say, very focused. It entered a state where It attempted to stretch through some rather nebulous planes or nebulous states to reach a firmer or more clearly defined state. And thus we find the Source, Itself, stretching forth through what has been called the astral plane. Through, in a specific sense, seven states within that level also. Reaching another specific division, and this division began again a seven-fold stretch into the more concrete orientation or frame or plane that we call physical existence.

Now is it not interesting that I have given you three sevens and yet, truly, there are four. Perhaps we will begin with these three and then explore the fourth one, the mental, more extensively than any of the others. I am, in a sense, saving the best to be discussed last.

In the first example, the seven-fold division is of what has been termed the spiritual plane. Many of you who read this know that Djwhal Khul has in his teachings this time simplified the approach. I commend him for his efforts. It helped truly for all to see the spiritual plane as containing what is called a monad, (the spiritual spark) and a soul - without considering another type of division. This division allowed you to see that the spiritual is much greater than previously considered and yet not become too intricately concerned about specific divisions that could distract from the goal.

I, Vywamus, now am framing existence from the Source's point of view at least as far as I can give you in my understanding. Thus we look now at the Source's unfoldment, Its seeking, Its focusing. And I seek to show you the true, from this point of view, unfoldment possibilities that the Source and its specific focuses are utilizing as a means of evolution.

Truly one must seek to go beyond any sort of a physical connotation as we reach this spiritual plane now. There is not at any division of the spiritual plane any sort of a physical sensation. There is not speech, smell, hearing, taste, feeling in the physical sense. There are some equivalents on the spiritual level. But one must let go as much as one can of the physical and see that *when one considers the spiritual, one is considering the Source's creative process*. When envisioned properly, this creative process can be equated to the creative principle itself. By that I mean *the Source is*. It always is seeking to be and to evolve and these highest seven states of being are more involved with the innate urge to be than with anything physical.

One might tend to ask, "Is this in the mental plane area, the thought process of the Source? Is this what we're dealing with here?" Not in the truest sense is that what I am discussing. When I said I would save the best for the last, I referred, truly, to the mental plane and its seven divisions. Those are perhaps for me the most illuminating in order to understand how all of existence is put together and how it works. Can you see that to look now in detail at seven times four - the four being the four planes - that this will give us a neat, detailed point of view of the Source. We should, it seems to me anyway, be able to stretch ourselves conceptually about the evolution of the Source Itself and self as a part of that Source.

Earlier I stated that the Source in an active state considered existence from a specific point of view,

4

and decided to explore in an encompassing manner that point of view. That is the beginning of a specific cosmic day, but it is much more basic than a thought process that I truly equated it to. It is again that creative urge to be, to explore and evolve. It is part of the nature of the Source Itself. Thus began this very basic activity of creating a cosmic day. In a sense before this beginning, there was a beginning in which the Source decided, framed in all cosmic days to be, and assigned specifics to explore during each cosmic day. This cosmic day the specific that the Source is exploring is "courage."

I told you the way that the Source goes forth, going from one level and leaving a specific pattern, stretching forth to the next, leaving a pattern of Itself, stretching forth to the next and leaving a pattern of Itself. Now not all parts of Itself are sounded forth simultaneously. By that I mean they are there potentially but they are not yet active because there is an ongoing wave; and at any specific point there are ever new parts of Itself being sounded forth. Thus the evolution of Itself is always occurring at all points of development. And this is important because the Source learns and grows and becomes in a balanced manner from a complete, encompassing view of evolution, through the particular specific that is being explored in any particular cosmic day.

Let us say that many specific parts of the Source, divine sparks truly, have gone from the seventh level to the first level of the next plane of experience (the mental) because the Source goes forth through seven levels of the spiritual plane, seven levels of the mental plane, seven levels of the astral plane and in a sense seven levels of physical possibilities. Let us say after leaving Its pattern on all seven levels of the the spiritual, the mental, the astral and on the physical, a divine spark has stretched forth as far as physical existence at this time allows, as far as the unfoldment of the particular cosmic day allows.

Then that divine spark, as it begins its evolution or return to the spiritual, begins to activate the divine possibilities or what I have called energy patterns that it left at each level as it passed through in the process of involution. On the third level of the physical, the spark turns around into what we call evolution, which is the invocation to activate the next pattern, the next level. Thus in physical existence while on the third level, the process of evolution leads one to activate the energy pattern on the fourth level. This level becomes available to that divine spark while still in physical existence. The process of going to the fourth level begins to activate, to invoke the fifth level and when this level has been fully attained, it is begun with the sixth level and so forth.

When the divine spark has again reached the seventh or the highest level that is physical, something very interesting happens. The process through physical existence has taught the divine spark a great deal and it begins to see truly from this point of view that it has energy patterns on every level, that it is all of these levels including the Source level and it begins to see that it does not need the illusion, the non-firm contact of the astral. Now,

6

before that time the astral level is used as an inner reference point for those in the physical when they are sleeping. Truly, every one believes that they need sleep or this contact with the astral to survive, up until about the fifth level. When one is standing at the threshold beyond which is all of the cosmos, all of existence beyond the physical, for a while this illusion of the astral may loom there. But as one breaks through to the seventh level, one begins to see, much more than before, the totality of self. In a sense, one goes again to the beginning level on the mental plane although one may have been exploring it much more extensively, and one returns as well to probably about the third level of the spiritual.

Now what about the first and the second levels of the mental? They are being explored at the same time that one explores the fifth and the sixth physical levels and usually the corresponding astral levels. You can see that it is not an either/or situation. And thus we are generalizing here when we say that one explores a specific level spiritually while exploring a specific level physically. There are always exceptions to every rule; such as in the case of those who have broken through rather rapidly in their awareness, thus attaining another level in what is sequentially a shorter period of time. I would say that the soul level could be equated to what I am terming the first and the second level of the spiritual plane.

The following is a way in which one might describe the various levels within each of the planes:

PHYSICAL PLANE

Levels 1-2

This vibration is utilized as a turnaround, anchoring point. The vibration is rather heavy in nature and cannot be sustained by the incarnating divinity while in a physical structure.

Level 3

The point during which involution becomes evolution. A penetration into existence that sharpens divinity's involvement in matter and which is explored until the invocation has begun at the fourth level to begin the evolutionary process.

Level three is the physical doorway, if you will, the physical point beyond which there is a heavier, non-physical vibrational pattern that anchors and pulls.

Each incarnating divinity reaches the third level and from this level, explores, in consciousness only, the first and second level. An exception would be those who choose (consciously) a cut-off state from divinity allowing a bridging to take place between the first and second physical level and the first and second astral levels. It is possible for such divine "renegades" to become lost in this vibrational area that never was meant to be bridged by two planes of existence. Therein I tell you something new that has not generally been given. If one can reach these beings and allow the physical part of their existence to begin to invoke the higher level, it will break that bridge and allow them to come forth from their self-exiled state.

Level 4

The level in which divinity experiences the "birth" of holistic seeing beyond the obvious. One becomes aware that there is much more than physical existence, that self is much more than just a physical being.

Level 5

The continuing development of the inner "sight" as the divine spark continues to integrate its perception beyond the physical.

Level 6

The point where one begins to glimpse universal concepts beyond the physical/self-centered approach that previously was needed as a tool, an impetus to evolution. This is recognized as the key point in complete unconditional service to the cosmic plan.

Level 7

At this point in its evolution, the divine spark is integrating the astral plane experiences into its physical framework and also launching self conceptually to approximately the third level of the spiritual plane.

It is, thus, a bridge to the complete unfoldment of the seven levels of the spiritual plane. Before this time, the first and the second levels of the spiritual plane were explored in conjunction with the physical. This means at this point one glimpses self as an extensive Source exploration vehicle. This glimpse is not only conceptual (in fact this concept may have been obtained much before this point), but is also realized to the point where one's service to the Cosmic Plan actually integrates this divine possibility.

In summing up the physical plane, it is a multi-leveled experience for allowing divinity to explore within a specific vehicle the going forth process which then becomes available as the returning or evolving process.

ASTRAL PLANE

Levels 1-2

A specific holding area where vibratory points are held that will later be reabsorbed by the Source.

Level 3

A nebulous, heavy vibratory area that varies as the physical correspondent which is its polarity varies.

Level 4

The specific point wherein the next physical events that have been created through the mass consciousness await in a formative state. Some of these events are then invoked by the third and fourth physical levels. Some are and some are not invoked but all potentials which may be invoked are contained at this level.

Level 5

Also contains some higher physical possibilities that can be invoked from the fourth and sometimes fifth levels of the physical plane.

Levels 6-7

Specific points where, while exploring physical existence, one studies with spiritual beings while the body sleeps. These two levels and part of the fifth truly are the ones that you may remember from a dream in which you have attended a class or seen a specific spiritual teacher.

The higher astral is a meeting ground for the specific purpose of instruction of some sort. It contains the vibrational stretching capabilities that enhance its use for this purpose. Many beings spend extensive periods, not of time but of focus of energy, in these higher levels. Their use is perhaps most appropriate for those who have not yet developed their "inner sight" as extensively as they will when they reach the sixth and seventh levels on the physical plane. These highest astral levels are always available to those who seek spiritual attunement by invoking the higher levels of the spiritual plane. One never, in a sense, grows beyond them. They are used as a teaching facility.

MENTAL PLANE

The mental plane is truly the creative plane. It is the one upon which the specific vibrations travel to create the evolution of the Source. We may look at it on a number of levels, in a number of ways, focusing on its specific attributes in rather an extensive way. But to begin our discussion of it let us first give you the information on levels one through seven that we can then refer to in interpreting the levels of the other planes.

Level 1

A focus in which the creative energy gathers up its potentiality. The focus stirs up the energies of creation, the expectancy that creation will now begin. It is the energy that gathers the beginning of the creative process.

Levels 2-3

These mental focuses are the creative process as it goes forth to meet what it has invoked. The creative processes have established a specific vibrational pull and the creative energies go forth now to fulfill that self-creative urge. If this sounds like a circle, it truly is. It means that the means to create are ever present because you have invoked the means to create from other creative efforts whether on this level or another. On the second and third level the mental is divided into the subconscious and the conscious mind. The creative endeavor is invoked mainly from the subconscious part of self at this level.

Level 4

This is the beginning of the synthesis of the subconscious and the conscious minds, the mental joining together as one seeks to fulfill one's potentialities by creating the service vehicle. Self creates, and it becomes capable at this point of working much more clearly for the cosmic unfoldment of the Source.

Level 5

More and more synthesis is being gained and the mental abilities now are of a potency that goes much beyond the rather automatic processes heretofore created without such integrative efforts. This level is the highest that is available for those who are still experiencing physical existence. Now, that does not mean that if a spiritual teacher decides to come to the Earth, he cannot use a higher level on the mental plane. But it is true for those who are still needful of evolution within a physical structure.

Level 6

One who functions on the mental plane at this level gathers truly large quantities of energy in preparation for the final level where the mental activity will be completely Source-oriented. One at this level sees the mental implications of any situation on a vast scope or scale because one is able to synthesize, project and evaluate the whole in an almost unlimited manner. This ability is a key to launch such a great one to the final or seventh level.

Level 7

The level of mental activity of those that represent and implement creation for the Source.

SPIRITUAL PLANE

Levels 1-2

These equate to what Djwhal Khul has called the soul level and what is called one's higher self in the part that is available to those focused in physical existence. Spiritual levels truly are, one might say, a purer focus, less interpretively linked to separation or differentiation.

Level 3

A specific point invoked/activated after extensive exploration of levels one and two. A joint checkpoint that concentrates what has been a "far-flung" effort to do what? At this point, one realizes absolutely the unity, the harmony, the blended quality of divinity's directional movement as it goes forth and brings back the realized state. The precise understanding of how to create this unity is beginning to be invoked at this level. It is stirring here.

Level 4

A point at which one is a focal point for great synthesizing possibilities or where one begins to work creatively with divine blueprints, divine unfoldment on a scale that begins to approach the universal.

Level 5

At this level the synthesis of divine possibilities on the universal scale continues. Perhaps some specialized training is begun after the basics have been developed. The universal intelligence factor is developed here to the point where nothing ever, ever, ever is separate. At this point one realizes that what has been termed"separateness" is never again possible.

Level 6

At this point, about which I am now giving my theory only, one addresses specific focuses within the Source much beyond any current evolvement. This means once again that synthesis into the oneness has allowed that oneness to share divine possibilities and they are then being explored much beyond any present level. Those who have not yet attained this level will explore the present specifics but a great one operating at this sixth level in purposefully going forth will allow the invocation of great Source potentialities to reference those potentialities. At this point that great one invokes a pattern on future potentialities for the Source Itself.

Level 7

Although long ago all illusion of separateness was gone, at this level the Source Itself stands before us, undifferentiated in any form that words can indicate. One operating at this level is simply a part of

Source that has Source responsibilities and Source abilities.

CHAPTER 2

WHY YOUR SEARCH IS IMPORTANT NOW

Mankind in his unfoldment, in his evolution, is doing well. Sometimes that is difficult to see, to realize, but it is true, nevertheless. Mankind is part of a multiplicity of forms in physical existence, meaning that physical life is manifesting on many levels. We have divided it into different kingdoms, if you will, the mineral, the vegetable, the animal, the human, and also what has been called the soul kingdom. That is quite interesting when you consider it. It means the unfoldment of physical life can truly evolve to the point where it no longer seeks such physical manifestation.

What happens then? What does this mean? Let us explore it now, together. Within the planet's hierarchical government are some who are now reaching a critical point in their evolution. They are now, many of them, realizing that any sort of physical existence must now be left behind. They have finished with it even from a teaching standpoint. The only exceptions will be in their "future" when the call goes out and they choose for a specific period to return as a stimulus to raise a physical planet to a new level such as is happening right now on the Earth.

Many of the teachers in the Hierarchy are completing their service. Thus, in the New Age on the Earth will be many new teachers that have specific purposes with the Earth at its New Age level. Others that are here now will not be present in the New Age. They will have chosen to experience and serve at a different focus. Now as you approach this point, you let go completely, my friends, of the needs of your individuality. This does not mean that the individuality is lost. It means that it is, again, perceived within the multiplicity of the Wholeness that does not reference self. Of course, it is understood that this focus that we call our individuality exists. But its needs have only to do with Wholeness and purposefully implementing the forward or evolving movement of the Creative principles.

As one reaches that complete dedication, creativity is enhanced and is understood more and more completely. Does this not say that those who are now going from the physical environment to a new level are thus becoming involved in a very basic sense with creating the evolution of existence, itself? To me, it does. Although one that is focused within a specific level, on a physical plane, may get a glimpse of the whole picture, it is not until beginning to launch self beyond physical existence, that one gets the whole panorama. One begins to glimpse, at least, what self and the creative principle have to do together. One sees ever more clearly the creative principle working in a multiple and far-reaching manner, and begins to glimpse how each point, how each little bit of creativity fits in with each other point of creativity.

I will discuss the creative principle in as simple a manner as possible, knowing that creative principles are multiple, are complex, are layered, are interacting, are intertwined, are much more than we can, any of us, conceive of right now. But, by separating our concepts and by intermingling them, I feel we can achieve our purpose of aiding understanding.

Let us begin then talking about the Creative Principle. We have equated the Cosmic Day to a poem that has been sounded forth by the Source Light. But how does this work? What do I mean, "sounding forth?" The Creative Principle works as follows: From the Wholeness, from the center that we call the Source, goes forth a pulse, a vibration. As it sounds forth, or from a physical viewpoint - moves - it stimulates the expansive Whole through which it "moves." The magnetic effect of such a creative principle at its highest level begins to attract an active principle to the whole conceptual framework of existence that has been sounded forth. This active principle then divides into two and it becomes thrusting on one hand and more receptive on the other. The male and female principles are thus "born."

This is the beginning. The creative desire to express and to experience has caused an activization process. The creative concept has been born. Now this creative process that has begun is still a potentiality, but the potentiality is active. It begins to explore its potentiality which is everywhere because this is a beginning. It has been sounded forth, but it is yet waiting to begin a more focused and many faceted expression of itself.

This creative urge of the Source is unlimited, unending, unreserved. It is eternal, all encompassing, and it moves and stimulates itself. You could say it is self-serving in the highest sense, in that it becomes its potential, and thus, moves its potential to another level, ever becoming, ever moving. The very fact of its activation brings forth yet another potential that, in a sense, has always been there, but yet, becomes and grows, is and was, and will be, and potentially, is realized.

Now for some of you, this may not be clear. But for others, your knowingness and intuition will recognize it. The potential for everything is always there, always will be, always has been. That must be perceived as part of what we might call the "mystery" of the Source, Itself. Because, before anything was, there was a sense, a potentiality for what was to be. Before the potentiality there existed the Source's desire. The Source was. It saw. It began. It became. It is the Source. Its essence spoke and all of creation began. Before its desire brought forth the beginning, It already was. It was, however, potential only.

Before it was even potential, what was there? Many have asked this. Many have contemplated it. I say to you, there was a potential for potentiality. You could carry that back, in a sense, evermore, until you reached a point that we could call a beginning of this particular level. It means, of course, that there

21

have been other levels of our Source. It, in my opinion, is but a mere hint of a much larger and more encompassing potentiality. Who is to say how many levels, how many potentialities exist as we seek ever an understanding of what began, of what was? In my opinion, my friends, one could go eternally through this process of potentialities. One must recognize that there never was a beginning in a static sense. The new beginning, as stated before in my teachings, is ever present and ever will be.

Let us return now to the point at which the Source has sounded forth and is experiencing the potentialities. The division has been made into the active thrust and passive reception modes of exploration. At this point the creative principle begins to explore through a divided focus. This does not mean that it does not come together. It does. But it also has specialized its efforts to become more cognizant, more intensely focused. It also helps to balance, to harmonize the sounding forth by such a division.

We are still at the very beginning. As the Source begins to express the creative surge, we are at but the origination of what we might call the river known as the creative flow. At the mouth of the river we can take two routes. The creative force does. But it also, as I stated before, mingles. There are purposes for which the creative principle must use both streams, both points of reference in order to create the most encompassing and appropriate connective link.

Creation continues within the whole conceptual framework. The creative force has stimulated an active state. As the creative force passes through all of this conceptual framework which is already active, its magnetic quality attracts and brings forth what has already been conceptualized. One must see that a conceptual framework has set up all potentialities and all that is needed is the creative force, through its magnetic and also electric qualities, to bring forth from this active potential what is already there. It stimulates and allows the unit of intermingling energy in its various forms or, before that, its various flows as is appropriate for its level, its focus within the framework of all of creation. Each specific focus in the conceptual area is stimulated by the active creation of the framework and the creative principle moving through it allows what has been potential and active to become fully a part of creation.

Various levels, various complex methods are utilized. In order not to overwhelm you with long words, I will just say because the creative principle on various levels contains the magnetism, the radiating, the electrical components that intermingle and interact, this leads each specific focus within the conceptual framework to respond exactly at the level that is needed to bring forth its full potentiality. Now, I do not mean that full potentiality is instantly realized on all levels. A gradual unfoldment by the creative forces itself, its insertion into the active potentiality, is appropriate.

As the creative thrust begins to realize its potentialities, a specific change begins to take place. Its potentiality divides. The receptive part of this thrust is added, multiplied, divided, subtracted by the creative process. What does that mean, exactly?

I am attempting to equate the next step as the creative thrust moves forward to a launch, a launching process, truly. Now what happens during a launch? We will equate it to a physical launch at this point. One thrusts forward. One loses the physical position that is subtracted. One adds thrust. One multiplies velocity. So you see, you subtract, you add, you multiply and you divide. How does one divide in a launch? You divide as the focus of the thrust becomes diversified.

Perhaps understanding that the creative thrust seeks its own magnetic/electric intensification through a multiple factoring system will help clarify my words. Intensifying anything leads to a multiplication factor that, in turn, may be divided to create a more encompassing and spreading awareness by the totality that we call the Source Light, Itself. Thus I am saying that this magnification which is created by the Source Light results in a radiating effect, which, as it radiates, sets up the magnetic attraction that becomes a cycle for creating an ever expanding multiplicity. The creative process, itself, is expanded in a sense by its own efforts and the way that it references the potentialities of itself.

Now to explain this in simpler terms, let us go once again to a musical instrument, let us say, an organ. The Cosmic Day begins with a specific intonation, a specific pattern of sound. Each note is sounded, blended, expanded, noticed and related within the range that is to be explored. After an all-encompassing view of the tonal pattern, the creative process begins to embellish the tonal exercise; to expand beyond the basic pattern of sound that has been created; to reflect the sound, the tone, to other levels; to harmonize with related patterns; to extend the potentials through the concepts that are gained and enlarged as the pattern of sound is realized. Thus the interrelatedness of the vibration, itself, leads to the necessary extension of the conceptual area by which the creative framework is ever moved forward.

One could say that there is a basic pattern, vibration, at the beginning of a Cosmic Day. But by the end of the Cosmic Day, it has been embellished, expanded, repeated, increased, intensified, explored on a multiple of levels and in the most comprehensive manner that is possible. The Source Light has taken a basic premise on a specific Cosmic Day and explored it as completely as its conceptual abilities can stretch, can magnify, can multiply, can radiate and then magnetically stimulate. The sound goes forth. It is utilized to create an encompassing and ever diversifying creation that, thus, realizes its own ever increasing comprehension and potentialities.

As the creative process becomes ever more multi-leveled and multi-layered, more reflection and more reflective levels are activated. The experiencing must be referred to a single focus that radiates to all of this multi-leveled multiplicity. We might equate its formation to that of a wheel. There is a hub.

From the hub, the spokes radiate outward and the rotation of the wheel allows that which began in the center to rotate, to evolve, to grow, to become, to reflect - from what it was - its new understanding and realizations. The creative force is multiplied as it goes forth. It becomes an ever expanding potential of what it has been. It seeks its own magnification. It learns. It participates. It listens. It becomes. It is.

The creative force may be studied. It may be viewed from any particular focus within its own evolvement. I, Vywamus, in my desire to understand have really specialized in the creative force. I am ever seeking to increase my own understanding of it. Thus I will share my perceptions with you. I am sure that as I continue my studies, I will enlarge my comprehension of the creative force and then I will share my new perceptions. But, we will work from where we currently are and seek further understanding.

To me, the most important point to realize about evolution is that it always expands you, that you may realize continuously, that the more encompassing your understanding is, the more there is to understand, that truly for you and for me our evolution has only begun. We need to continue to seek clarification of our understanding of the creative force and to learn from and about it because it contains many levels, many centers and many unexplored points.

On the earth, you utilize time to organize the process of your evolution and learning. You may not have thought about time in this manner, but it truly is given to you on the physical level as a tool, as a means to discover. At the same time you are learning, of course, the Earth learns also, and each learning opportunity becomes a means of identifying the next step to be learned.

Right now, here on your earth, the next step is really very clear, at least, I believe that it is. The Earth is seeking to allow itself and all of its parts (each one of you) to be allowing and trusting of each other, to have confidence in each other, to express unity through the love - centered approach to life.

The time is now to discover who you are. Now to grow into a more allowing point of view. Now to see how you may trust everyone without an out-of-balance state coming forth when you seek to do so. Now to utilize your many abilities and strengths. Now to guide others and be supportive of them. Now to acknowledge your Divine heritage and your awakening understanding. Now to begin to sort through things, to understand, to let go of what is no longer serving you well as you do sort, and to let in those strengths and abilities that are beginning to be seen by you. Now to serve unconditionally. Now to understand the group process and your part in it. Now to say to self, "Yes, I agree the nowness is the key to the light that I am seeking now."

Your earth senses the availability of this nowness point of view and it awaits each one of your realization points, your clearing, and your growing understanding.

For the earth, then, the timing of your search is absolutely vital. The nowness in the evolution of the earth states "I seek now and am discovering the beauty, love, allowingness and support within that seeking process. I will return in full measure what I discover through my search. I return it to the Whole, with my love, now."

CHAPTER 3

BECOMING AWARE - THE SELF DISCOVERY PROCESS

As evolution ever moves forward, Divinity expands its awareness in whatever focus it may be experiencing. Perhaps you have not considered this fact: that because of evolution, the constant expansion of Divinity's awareness makes possible an ever expanded program of existence. Consider then the following: Divinity, the Source, the Originator, began. The beginning is but a specific point in existence and does not necessarily mean there was nothingness before it. But it was a very special focus for experiencing. We could say that at the beginning the Source's, the Creator's, awareness reached a point where visibly it was possible to see the expansion of existence.

That is an interesting statement and you might want to ponder it. At this point of focus, the expanding of awareness was discernible. I use that word very carefully, meaning that everyone, everything is a specific focus of the Oneness and as such expresses Divinity in a unique and individualistic manner. But one specific that is always present with each individual focus of Divinity is this: there are points of new beginnings, and that is definitely plural, at which time one can view the result of much seeking, much learning. The teachers have equated this to reaching a new level of understanding.

Many of you have had such experiences. You struggle and you learn and you suddenly, it seems to you, become aware of life in an entirely new manner, much expanded, much more free flowing. Is it sudden? I do not think so. The ever expanding spiral of evolution has just become visible.

Does this say, going back to the Source Itself, that it has been experiencing forever and that at one specific point or focus, It became visible? In my opinion, it does. Now, in your individual case, this is important. It means that as you learn and as you seek, that you need not really be discouraged. That everything you are seeking will become visible at a certain point of awareness. There is no doubt, there is no way that you can avoid it. You couldn't if you tried.

Thus, if you are seeking more abundance, know this, that although you are working hard to achieve it and cannot perhaps see the results right now, when you become aware enough by the specific tools and methods that you are using to aid self, you will see the abundance, it will become visible, and you cannot miss it. Because the ever expanding consciousness of self will, at a particular point of evolution, notice what is already there. This does not negate at all, and please do not misunderstand me here, the value of working with methods that specifically address blocked areas, because those methods are very helpful in allowing awareness to come forth more quickly.

But as I view now those who are seeking and working very hard and cannot yet see the results, I say to each of you, "Yes, I, Vywamus, assure you, my friends, that at a specific point, that for many of you is very close in your awareness, you will notice everything that you are seeking. It will be there because when you so notice it, it is manifest in your life.

I am now discussing awareness, and, of course, everyone is seeking greater understanding of Divinity, basically. This is our journey, this is what all of us desire and strive for, more than anything else. For some there is not yet a conscious recognition of this goal. Others are very aware of it and journey forth with gladness and with joy, feeling very privileged to be doing so.

I, Vywamus, am one of the latter, and really do appreciate the journey. My friends, your elder brothers, now, the teachers, the members of the Hierarchy, understand perhaps a little more clearly than you the journey. Welcome them into your life, appreciate their help and their, perhaps, slightly clearer perception of what is basically being sought. They are clearer on living. They are more cognizant of the opportunity to serve and to bring forth the Creator's Cosmic Plan. They have let go of the personality needs, the ego has completely been assimilated within the soul level.

You see, my friends, their will now is completely aligned into service. Service for them, and I am talking about the government of the planet, the spiritual government that guides humanity, means that they view all of the Earth as Divinity's way of expressing and they seek always on a large and extensive level to aid humanity. That does not mean that there aren't guides, that there are not rules, that there are not universal laws that must be respected, there are. The most important one is, of course, free will.

In looking at the Earth, we the Spiritual Teachers, notice what has been created. That is not at all a negative statement. Humanity has understood much, has learned a great deal. And, if sometimes in its learning experience, it expresses physically some frustration, some less than perceptive understanding of what physical existence means, the spiritual government knows that by aiding where allowed and by allowing the evolutionary spiral to do its work, by letting evolution work, my friends, the planet's consciousness will reach a specific point of awareness in which it sees more clearly what is the journey and what is the goal.

Earth living reflects all of what has been experienced on the Earth. And if we look at it in a comprehensive way, we can see in certain physical locations the results of much learning. That is not negative. It is a very positive statement. And I should note that I am talking about all the segments of the planet's consciousness. In other words, the level that we call humanity has certainly had an important effect on the Earth - but the animal, vegetable, and mineral kingdoms also share in the evolution of the planet.

The animal kingdom has guided the Earth at many particular points. Humanity does not always see this or know it. But sometimes when humanity is experiencing a block or an effect that they have created, such as a war or strife in any form, the animal kingdom has perhaps negated some of this effect, acted as a balance, as a harmonizing component in the consciousness of the planet. Certainly this is true. The great Divinity focus called the animal kingdom responds well to Wholeness, to Oneness. It really is more responsive to the Creator than humanity is.

Sometimes there has been, in one locality, great gatherings of birds, or great gatherings of herds of animals. Their sense of Divine purpose and in a basic way, of survival, bring them together to focus a needed balance in a specific physical location. This has taken place over the history of the Earth.

The vegetable kingdom of the planet Earth is so evolved, so perceptive, that it has negated many times effects that otherwise would have been rather catastrophic. At the time of Atlantis, the vegetable kingdom, by its perceptive understanding, aided the Children of the Light.

At the time of Atlantis there was a specific focus of separation that had been manifested on the Earth, meaning that those who had misconstrued what Divinity's purpose is, and who had allowed their

33

own wants, needs and desires to guide them, were seeking to overcome the Earth. One specific way in which the vegetable kingdom (all of the beautiful plants and flowers) aided Earth there - was through utilizing the fragrance of a beautiful flower within the temples to attune specifically to Divinity. One could not help but experience a closer attunement to Divinity when this fragrance was present.

Now one can, if one desires, choose negative attunement. The separate ones certainly were not greatly affected by even this wonderful fragrance. But those that perhaps wavered, did not see clearly enough to know which choice to make, were aided to make the right choice, to stand with the Children of the Light when encountering this fragrance, this specific attunement to Divinity.

This is but one of multiple ways in which the vegetable kingdom has partaken in harmonizing and, for those who look for logical proof, validating that there is an essence, there is a guidance from something that one cannot see physically. To me, seeing the beauty of the Earth as viewed through the vegetable kingdom is validation of Divinity. This is proof that Divinity's expression may be harmonious.

The mineral kingdom expresses on a physical plane Divinity at a very basic and important level. Within it are many different focuses from grains of sand to beautiful, stunning crystals. There are many, many differences of focus within that Oneness that we call the mineral kingdom. As evolution takes place this specific physical manifestation of Divinity evolves, grows and becomes. As it changes, we see many changes occur on the physical Earth. These come about through the expansion of consciousness in the mineral kingdom.

What I am really seeking to convey here is that within this Wholeness, this Oneness we call the physical planet Earth, there are specific blends of consciousness that the Creator, that Divinity expresses in as many ways as one can possibly conceive of, and the mineral, the vegetable, the animal, the human, and the spiritual government or soul levels are only some of the ways. It is much more complex than this. This is one way to look at evolution.

Now it will aid your understanding to know that evolution does truly begin, sound forth, emanate forth, from the Oneness. It does not ever leave the Oneness, but it becomes more, it extends beyond that perception that it has had that we call the Oneness. It goes forth and it evolves and it becomes. It does not do so in just one specific way, so to frame it in one way and say, "this is the way that evolution works," allows you to see only a part of the picture.

You may certainly look at any one part and say, "This is how evolution works in this particular instance or focus," knowing that you are always going to encounter different focuses and different methods through which the Creator, the Divinity, experiences.

Recognize that you do encounter these differences in perception of how evolution works. Be joyful, be appreciative, because in each one you have discovered another focus. You have increased your understanding, you have learned, you have expanded your awareness. Do not discard the fact that there are approaches that may be different from your perception of how Divinity expands and evolves. Gather them up, seek them out. Do not say there is just one way, my friends.

I will now discuss awareness from the perspective of transformation. Awareness is the recognition of the level of creativeness that one sees within self. This means of course that although each Divine spark is complete, is a whole - that to fully utilize, to fully engage potentialities, one must be aware of self AS those potentialities.

At the beginning of any Cosmic Day, the Source level begins an active state. Specifics within it are activated in a harmonious manner. Within a conceptual framework, the Source literally begins to play upon this vibrational framework which has been sounded forth. Each particular vibration within that framework is unique, not isolated nor separate, but a part of the Whole; having its unique function, having its unique rhythm, having its unique role. The interrelatedness (interaction) of each unique perspective/part on every level begins to light up the whole conceptual vibratory framework so that evolution or Self-discovery may take place. This is a rhythm - a vibrational flow - that is sounded forth. One must see, understand, then, the nature of such a vibrational flow to become aware of how the process of Self-discovery occurs. In the pulsing, or rhythm of the sounding forth process, is what is termed a "frequency," meaning a repeating pattern of activity and then an equally important inactive or pause between such active periods.

Existence, then, or what has been termed "evolution", occurs in the following manner; the Source in its interrelatedness becomes active. After this active period, there is an inactive period in which the Source reflects upon what has been stimulated. The active phase has been termed a "Cosmic Day," the inactive or reflective phase has been called a "Cosmic Night."

Because of the nature of the Source, each Divine spark contains all potentialities of the Source itself. It also participates within existence and evolution in the same manner as the Source itself. Thus, a Divine spark who is sounded forth on a Cosmic Day as an integral part of the Whole, an interrelatedness of the Whole, functions actively or enters the active state of the pulse, of the vibrational thrust, with interim periods of inactivity or reflection. Both phases of the pulse are equal in the sense of expressing the Divine. Both the active and passive allow evolution to take place.

Each vibration or Divine spark has its individual rhythm within the Whole. The Whole expresses, remember, by its interrelatedness on every level. Some Divine sparks will be active on a specific Cosmic Day while others remain inactive. The "positioning" within the Whole changes as each spark literally seeks its own full potential and, at the same time, through the marvelous manner in which everything fits together, each spark as it evolves fulfills the needs of the Whole.

One might use the example of a beautiful piece of music which is being played. The conceptual whole is there - the piece of music is complete - but as it is played, certain specific notes are active, are focused upon, while others express the inactive or reflective state. Again, one is not more important than the other and they truly do complement each other. The active and inactive phases give a sense of proportion to the Whole as it seeks and learns.

Why discuss this at all? How does this relate to transformation? Let us continue and I will clarify the matter. Our music of the Whole has been sounded forth. Some notes or vibrations are active while others are inactive. At a specific point, certain parts of the Whole encounter what has been termed "physical existence." The Divine vibration, the Divine spark that enters physical existence encounters a specific vibration which resonates, which reflects deeply or has what one might term a mirror effect within the Whole.

What I am saying here is that when you as a Divine tone enter physical existence, it - meaning the vibrational level of physical existence itself - in its interaction with your specific vibrational level, creates what I have termed a MEANS TO MIRROR BACK TO SELF WHAT YOU ARE CREATING. Thus, by using the mirror, you can gain a more complete understanding of self and how you fit into the Whole. This is important and I ask you to consider it carefully.

The transformational process, then, is simply this: the means to discover in physical existence who you really are. You become CONSCIOUS, through the mirroring process while in physical existence, that you are an evolving being. You discover through interaction with others, because they mirror to you your beliefs. Physical existence, then, is a major tool in the process of transforming self to that point of awareness which will gradually show you HOW you fit into the Whole and WHAT your responsibilities are within it. Thus, through physical existence you gain a true perspective of the nature of the interaction of the Whole. The vibrations in physical existence are clearly defined, are so definite, so specific that the mirroring effect is easily understood and allows assimilation within the creative process to take place.

During this transformational process, the first part of what one might call the "physical trip" focuses on self. The awareness is centered within what is termed the "personality/ego." One views existence from a personality perspective given by the Creator for the purpose of developing a means of viewing, on the physical level, the life process. Much is learned/achieved during these early physical experiences. One learns to survive on the physical level. One learns that an active role in existence is essential for physical survival. One interacts with others, accepts certain responsibilities, makes specific commitments. Thus, through experiencing which is played out in a panorama of roles in a theater called "physical existence," one views what takes place from the point of view of the personality. More and more potentials within self are activated. Great strengths become readily available for usage. Focuses into lifetimes of special abilities are made. Gradually, the personality level becomes strong, independent, able and, in the sense of what it is, mature.

At this point, the evolutionary process seeks to connect beyond the physical level. The means to do so is called the soul level. Although, of course, this level of awareness has been present all along, it truly has not yet been utilized in a comprehensive manner in physical existence. The strong personality has literally attracted its attention, has literally called to it and said, "Yes, I have become so strong that the framework has been created for you now." Of course, the personality level will not recognize that this invocation has been made to the soul, but the soul responds, seeing - becoming very excited about - this opportunity to pursue its Divine purposes in physical existence.

The soul recognizes that physical existence is not "less than." It sees physical existence as an important assignment in which to serve, through which to learn and grow!

What is necessary, then, to move beyond this personality/ego focus? How does one transform self to the next available level in your evolution? First, it is necessary to see that, in the fullest sense, it is the evolution of the Whole and our part in it that we are discussing. If you view evolution from only the perspective of self at the personality level you see but a one-point focus of the Whole. The nature of the transformational process, then, is allowing/accepting the viewpoint of Wholeness within self. Now, you have been told this over and over, but perhaps the following example will make it clearer.

As an example, then, let us view a physical group which comes together for the purpose of service or to aid others. Each member of the group adds strengths and abilities to this purpose of aiding others. Each adds a specific vibration or rhythm that, when coming together within the group, creates the rhythm or pulse of the Whole. As one views the group purpose, seeking to implement the service goal of aiding others, it becomes absolutely necessary for each member of the group to also see, appreciate and allow the perspective of all the other group members. When every point of view is thus expressed and then INTERACTS with every other point of view, what comes forth through the group effort is evolution of the purposeful coming together of the group, which in the case of our example, is aiding others.

In order to bring forth a clear, comprehensive goal, then, it is necessary for each group member to contemplate/learn through what the group has discovered together. THIS IS TRANSFORMATION! The ability to use the learning process of the Whole.

During physical existence, achievement becomes a means to interact with life in a manner which is satisfying and fulfilling or what has been called a means to be "happy." If one runs a race and wins, the experience of winning allows a specific focus or contact point within the Whole to be reached.

In the active portion of evolution as the Whole thrusts forward, there is always a particular focus that leads the forward movement. In physical existence it would be called "first." Thus, in our example of a race, the one who comes in first achieves for a brief moment that contact into the Whole he is seeking. There is a lot of energy at this stimulating point which is utilized by many as their only means of bringing energy to their creative process. Thus, they seek, sometimes desperately, to be "first" in all endeavors, to gain the necessary stimulation, the necessary energy connection.

Within the foregoing lies a false premise and it is this. You cannot ACHIEVE your Divine connection. You already HAVE it, given to you as a gift by the Creator: You DO need to ACTIVATE from the potential to the realized state all of what has been so given. Achievement, then, is for the purpose of evolving the potential into the realized! As we seek each point of realization, we must seek to recognize that sometimes we will be "first," but because of the pulse of existence, we must also at times be "last," which truly is not a less desirable positioning within the Whole!

We see, then, that through the process called trans-formation, we will discover our "place" and that that place is always becoming clearer, is always changing and will involve us in awareness levels that are ever more cosmic. How exciting! How wonderful! Look forward to this eternal journey with joy, my friends. It is a pleasure to be traveling with you now!

Now as you begin to realize that physical existence is truly an opportunity for a spiritual being to be-come, to unfold, the emotional body responds in a very positive manner. This means the joy level comes forth and you feel, perhaps, happier than ever before. Truly, then, a clearer use of the emo-tional body is stimulated through the sense that something real within you has been contacted.

What does this mean and am I saying that if you are not joyful you have not contacted something real? Of course not. But, I am saying that reality for each of you has certain signposts or points, in-dicators if you will, which when recognized will show you that your life is perhaps much more "tuned in" to your ideal or to the Cosmic Plan that you may have noticed!

The emotional body, the appreciation factor of the Source, is one such indicator. By being honest with self and seeing what each emotion is stimulating and connected to, you can see self's positioning on this highway of awareness you are traveling.

Often, we have stated that pain, loss and trauma are attached to false beliefs. I wish to emphasize now that the reverse is true also. Joy, unconditional love, appreciation and true humility are attached to the realization process of formulating your own truth.

There is a lightening process, both in the sense of feeling lighter as you discover your true reality, or see your source-level abilities, and also a directional flow which has been called Cabalistically a "lightning flash" which truly integrates the flow of your energy when you allow and stimulate the ideal within self.

To explain that, let us say, for example, that you are a parent, and have given birth to a child. This little one, newly born on the physical plane, has the potential to live a full, productive life. You, as the parent, see the potential and during the growth process seek to guide the child, to direct the child's energy, if you will, into channels or ways which will create a life flow that has meaning and allows your child to enter what we might call the "full creative stream," meaning he will have the type of career and personal relationships that are fulfilling and satisfying.

To equate this child to a stream of energy at its beginning point, then, a sense of direction is made available from the parent or the Creator and the child sets forth to navigate/direct this stream of energy. Through a discovery process, the child gradually learns the most productive manner of navigating/directing the stream. Sometimes, the trial and error method leads to coming in contact with rocks or boulders or even the temporary loss of the means to navigate the stream, by which I mean the loss of the physical vehicle. You see, of course, that in this scenario here I am talking about more than one life, a series of lives in physical existence.

One's ideal direction, then, is attained through the discovery process, but it isn't necessary to break up on a rock before making a realization which will allow you to avoid that particular rock's impact upon self. The realization process, then, is such an alternative to the experiencing, over and over again, all of the rocks or boulders that have been gathered erroneously into one's stream.

Certainly it is important to have a means of identifying the areas which make up these rocks or boulders and we, your teachers, through you, our channels, are seeking to show you what events, both on the physical level and more cosmically, have created these misperceptions that are woven into your search now.

Certainly, your Divine Intent or your desire to aid the Whole, is the reason you are willing to keep moving your vehicle within this stream of energy that we call the Whole's evolution. You also recognize a deep desire to know, to become, that is literally built into you by the Creator's corresponding desire to know. The Source, then, in its discovery process, initiates this desire and each of us is the means to discover everything that is there to be discovered.

Each time, then, you discover something that shows you more clearly why you exist, who you are and what the purpose of your journey in awareness truly is, you become more able to navigate/direct your stream of energy, to use it more and more in line with your full co-creator abilities and to allow the creative process within self to be discovered with true wonder, appreciation and joy! It is this sense of wonder, then, that helps you to recognize the true miracle of creation, that helps you to see the broad sweep, the magnificent cosmic panorama that is unfolding all around you. It helps you to know beyond any previous doubt that the Divine is present, is living and creating on every level and is present within every being who exists. Truly, the discovery of the magic of existence prompts you to hurry forth, as you will not wish to miss discovering each new, exciting part of the creative process within your own life and within the lives of others. Enjoy, discover, play, become excited about your life and your future. It is a bright one indeed! You, as Creator, are a magnificent light-being of whom the Angels sing and whom the Cosmos salutes!

CHAPTER 4

ENERGIZING OPPORTUNITIES

Let us look at the creative process, seeking to understand the nature of it and seeking to recognize how the ideal is generated at the Source level. Let us also examine how each of us, in our desire to utilize our creative potential, gradually accepts the ignition process, which I will discuss next, as a means to generate the energy for self's creative efforts and, thus, to build, step by step, the means to journey forth.

In this Cosmic Day experience, you were given what I have called an energy pattern, an energy formula that contains the means to generate all that is needed, that is desired. The dynamic energy, or what has been called the male polarity within self, ignites the creative process. This ignition thrusts deeply into the energy that is receptive, the female energy, which has literally been receiving or gathering up the information, the learning, all that has been received during this particular means of expressing, whether we are speaking of a Cosmic Day or your present lifetime here on the Earth. Recognize that physical existence reflects your spiritual evolution and perceptions.

What does it mean, then, to ignite the creative process? How does this take place? To begin with, energy comes together or interacts; in a sense, it interlocks. As each type of energy is gathered, a message goes forth from the female invoking the ignition process. When the message becomes invocative on a great enough scale, then the dynamic energy is attracted by this invocation process.

If humanity had not become confused in the polarity area, at this point the male polarity would be interacting clearly with the female as her invocation in the gathering up process calls forth the male. However, because of an energy confusion that literally translates on the physical level to an energy "stuckness", the clear invocation to invite the ignition process (the dynamic male energies to interact with the female) is not made. Generally, and I am generalizing here, the receptive or female energies have not allowed contact with the male.

You may very well ask at this point, "how is that possible?" All of you here on the physical plane are living, you are creating your own lives. How is it possible that the interaction between the polarities has been cut off? Well, I am not saying that it has been completely cut off. But many have substituted the will aspect instead of using the male polarity in the ideal manner.

The will aspect has a dynamic flow. It is usually considered to be first ray energy, although there are some exceptions here. But, this dynamic flow of energy, the will aspect,when utilized as a substitute for the male polarity, creates from a forced perception. Not possible, then, is the ideal level of interaction with the two polarities, the male and the female, sharing the creative process. The will literally forces the female's participation in the joining process energywise. There is built into this interaction, which remember is not ideal, a resentment on the part of the female. She resents being used, being forced to partake in something in which she is not being given an equal opportunity to be that creative partner that her potential tells her is her ideal. Thus, we see that because the invocation from the female is confused, what she invokes instead of the male polarity is the will aspect that then makes her feel as if she has been used, mistreated sometimes, or at least not utilized within a full Divine partnership which is the ideal.

You have within self, in the polarity area, two Divine creative perspectives, one complementing the other. They are meant to be equal partners within the creative act. Their roles are not the same, remember, but they are complementary. However, when the female does not clearly understand how to utilize that naturally magnetic part of herself in a way that becomes invocative, then a basic component of the misperceptions that occur in the polarity area form.

A clear polarity area is essential to the use of your full, co-creator level abilities. Many of you at the human level have a rather complicated belief structure in this area. To give you an example, the female aspect is not just one perception within each of you. But, there may be as many as ten different perceptions or misperceptions within the female polarity concerning her role that need to be reconciled, resolved, integrated, or cleared. Not all of you have ten different perspectives but there are some of you that do.

The male polarity area is even more complex for most of you than the female. Recognize, of course, that each being that exists does have and utilize both types of energy, whether they are in a female or male body during this present lifetime. You really have both types of energy within self.

It is important, then, to look at what is being mirrored to you on the physical plane. If you are married or in a polarity relationship, look at what your relationship partner is mirroring to you. What you see through this mirroring are your own beliefs in the opposite polarity area. Now, certainly we think of false beliefs but look also at the strengths, at the beauty, at the understanding that is present there. Look, then, at your relationship partner to see what you have learned, what you understand and what you believe about the opposite polarity.

It is no accident, of course, that most of you, at one time or another, experience polarity relationships within your lifetime. Even those of you who do not, have experienced them in other lifetimes. These relationships, then, are at the core of seeking to understand your creative process, your creative potential.

I have used the example of someone who has a relationship and loses it. Again, they have another relationship. This one ends. Over and over again, this pattern of behavior repeats, having a relationship and then losing it. What, then, is the basic cause for this pattern of behavior to be so ingrained within self? You may not recognize this pattern of behavior as yours. Let us say, for example, that you have been married to the same person for many, many years without loss. Know that to some extent or another you all have such a pattern. Recognize that you have had many, many relationship partners over the history of your lives on the Earth. The death process, then, seems to interrupt the maintenance of such relationships.

It is, then, to the nature of change that we must look here. We must seek to see that through change loss is not created, or an interruption of the creative goals that are being sought. Can you see this interruptive pattern? You may have a relationship, live within it for may years until the physical body ages. This aging process in itself seems to interrupt the seeking of creative goals. One "retires" and ceases to seek goals at some point within the physical life. Many of you have many times died "with your boots on," meaning there was no official retirement period. But, nevertheless, you all reached a point physically where you said, "I can't do it any more. I must cease to be as creative as I once was."

Built into the belief structure, then, is an obsolescence factor that must be removed, that you must see beyond. The aging process seems destructive with regard to relationships and, thus, to the creative process. A man, when he feels he is too old, is no longer able to have relationships with a woman. He has built into his belief structure this obsolescence factor then. If, and there are some that are able to do this, his beliefs are pretty clear in this area, he may be sexually active well into the 80's, 90's and some even at age 100 of your Earth years. You see, there really isn't any limitation, even in this area, unless you have, over and over again, reinforced it in your physical lives.

Most of you who are in a female body have said to self, over and over, life after life, "I must receive what is given to me, what is brought to me sexually. I have no choice in the matter. I am the receiver only." Now, gradually and in some of your lives, a few of you have allowed yourselves to be more active in your sexual role (and I don't mean running from partner to partner) meaning that within the receptive mode is an active state that is the means to create that equal partnership that all of you are seeking in the joining or coming together process. Until you, then, as a woman, accept your active role within this joining process, you will continue to feel "put upon" or forced in the very passive nature of the receptive mode without seeing that the integrating part of it is the active role that is your part of that igniting process of the joining or coming together, the sexual union, or, in a larger sense, the creative process itself.

In our work together in the Foundation, I, Vywamus, emphasize the polarity area. We are using symbols and many, many ways to promote an understanding of how creation takes place. We are literally taking the polarity area apart, piece by piece, and when we get all of those nuts, screws and bolts laid out there, then we will go to the Divine blueprint and put back all of the parts into the Divine pattern that is your goal. Certainly this may take us more than five minutes. In point of fact, this is the journey, your unfoldment of the creative process and all that it involves, all of its aspects. However, I do promise you this. I Vywamus, am going to keep digging around in the polarity area within those of you who come and ask me to aid them in order that you may establish a clearer means of understanding this rather complex and, yet, divinely simple area. It is simple in its conceptual view. The intricacies become evident when we view what many of you have done with it. Literally has the energy flow become confused, convoluted, stuck, webbed in, all of these terms that many of you are familiar with.

Your energy may be equated to a triangle. This triangle is a basic unit of the creative process and we can look at it in quite a number of ways. I am seeking, then, to show you that triangles are a basic unit of the creative process. In an effort to understand the polarity area, then, see a triangle, an equilateral triangle, and on the left, your female energies, on the right, your male energies, and on the base of the triangle is a combination of both. Seek to reach a centered point at the base of the triangle in order that the energies may go forth to that point of the triangle that we call the apex. When this takes place, the whole creative energy triangle is ignited, but it takes that balanced point, the interaction of the female and the male polarities, to contact the, let us say, full scope of creative potential that is available to each of you. If the contact point is not balanced and you get either too much female or too much male energy, then the ignition process is not complete, it is not aligned and it doesn't contact your potential.

Although what we see visually is that many of you do not know how to utilize your male energies completely, the basic reason for not reaching your potential in the creative process lies within the female or receptive stream of energies.

In order to understand this completely, I must take you to the Source level to that event which we call your birth or your assuming an active role within the Source. It has also been termed the point where you became individualized. To me, this event was when the Source said to you, "It is time now for you to actively take part in the creative process." Before that, you had been in what we call the undifferentiated Source, which is rather a womb-like state. Many of you were warm, happy, peaceful, and nothing was required of you. The Source literally knocked on your door one day (creating for you the door, first of all) and said, "It's time, little one. Now you go forth." Of course, it is important to recognize that you don't "go" anywhere. You simply activate a component of energy that, although potential, hadn't been active before. It is also important to recognize that we are talking much beyond sequential time; really there is a focus directed at the creative process and, thus, the adjustment of the creative process, through a focusing mechanism, became available to self.

When this "birth" takes place each being "reacts" to it a little differently. But, for all of us, there is some loss of what has been and some impact in the receptive energy area. For some, it is quite severe and some of you believe that this receptive mode and what comes through it is a violation of your free will. It seems to you, subconsciously, that you are forced to receive because in your active role for the Source you had no choice in the creative process.

Well, I am here to tell you that you did have a choice. All of you chose this coming forth process. Some do not agree to it and, thus, remain within the undifferentiated Source eternally. All of you came forth through your own choice, but to some of you, that itself seemed forced. You felt, in a sense, that you were "between a rock and a hard place" in your coming forth process.

As we look deeply into some of these causal areas, recognize that I am generalizing in this material and each of you will need to be more specific in understanding the way you, personally, have woven your own truth about polarity.

Now, please do not misunderstand my words. With your divine intent you came forth lovingly, and willingly, but, sometimes, the subconscious creative process does not see clearly. There is a tendency, then, to accept as eternal a particular perspective that was received/brought forth from one particular event. That is why it is so very important to look deeply at this Source-level event called the individualization process. Recognize that the more honest you can be with yourself, the more you can look deeply into your own belief structure, the sooner you will begin to unravel, clarify this complex polarity area.

What we have here, then, is an energy formula, a dualistic stream of energy, the male-female, the receptive-dynamic. How can they interrelate clearly and, thus, allow through that acceptance of one another's potential, that igniting process which then allows a creative effort that you seek to manifest to be unified, integrated and Whole?

This, dear ones, is exactly what a Co-Creator learns to do with vast amounts of energy. He creates a balanced, dualistic stream that then unites over and over again in an eternally pulsating manner that step by step or level by level ignites the full effort that he is seeking to create or bring forth. This is the full spiral effect that is self-generating. What he does is get it started and set it up in such a balanced manner that its sparking and, therefore, its full usage is eternal. It must be adjusted to that exact point of balance, meaning that the two streams of energy must be precisely or exactly balanced. When this is accomplished, the Co-Creator can create these self-generating spirals that are maintenance-free and creative in their own right.

Think about it this way. Perhaps you have seen someone juggling ten plates. If you haven't, they are placed on ten sticks and one who has learned to spin the plate keeps going from one plate to another making sure that they remain balanced and rebalancing them, when necessary. Envision, then, the Co-Creator, who starts the creative spirals spinning with the full knowledge and understanding that enable this balance to be eternal without worrying, then, about having to go back and reanalyze or make the plate balance again. It is an exciting possibility to think about and you are ready. Each of you are seeking to discover who you are, and where you are, really, by using your receptive energies, and invoking a larger and more creative use of self on the physical plane.

All through this material I have been talking about the creative process and I am not using these words in a limited manner. I do not mean here only art and music, although they may be included in my meaning, but I mean the full use of the entire spectrum of your abilities which create a larger and more progressive use of yourself within the Cosmic Plan for the Earth.

The Cosmic Plan, dear ones, is a spiral of energy that was set in motion on a very cosmic level, indeed, stepped down, then, to physical existence by those of us who understood how to do this. It is a self-generating creative plan, but, perhaps, on the physical level, needs a little rebalancing now and then. In its spiritual ideal, it does not. But in the usage on the physical level, it needs monitoring and needs the creative input of you and all of those who are here on the Earth.

To me, one of the most exciting things about physical existence is this wide scale of possibilities and probabilities. Now, that may seem to you to be a strange statement. Many of you, and this always rather surprises me, seem to feel that the Earth isn't doing too well, that there are so many problems and so much trauma that it couldn't be what was intended. Well, yes, there is some non-clear usage of your planet. Certainly the Creator's Plan, the Cosmic Plan for the Earth, didn't include pain, trauma and many of the reactions and misperceptions that you see all around you. But, in the overall plan, these are relatively minor. When I look at you, each of you, what I see is a Divine being who is getting to be quite cosmic in your understanding and in your recognition of what it takes to be a good Co-Creator. Those of you who have merged with your soul, or who are approaching that point now, have the power of the soul available and this, dear ones, is awesome. It truly is. The souls have the means within them to finalize this chapter of Earth living that all of you are involved in now.

Within each of you, then, at soul level, is the key to understanding your creative process and, through a deep discovery of what the male and female stream of energy truly are, you can allow your energy format to approach its ideal flow. Any sort of flow that has been distorted can be realigned. I encourage you to work in the polarity area, going more and more deeply into it.

CHAPTER 5

ALLOWING THE EARTH TO STIMULATE YOU NOW IN YOUR EVOLUTION

You, my friend, have come forth, have individualized. You are Divinity experiencing. You will unfold the plan of Divinity in an ever more perceptive manner. When this is understood, one comes to the following conclusions: the purpose of the encompassing knowingness that we call the Creator or God, if you will, is the same as our purpose - there is no difference; we move forward in our perceptiveness to reach that perfect delicate point of balance where we may serve extensively, where we may create the perfect vehicle for the Knowingness to experience. In unfolding our creative abilities more and more, we input into this Knowingness our Perceptiveness, our Understanding. It seems to me that the sooner Earth beings, human beings, recognize the all-encompassing journey and its Purposes, the sooner they will be in the mode of experiencing that will make them "happy." Human beings seek happiness, but what they are really seeking is more Understanding. Understanding What? Understanding their own unique part in the unfoldment of the evolution of the All-Knowingness.

Now, this has been said before. It is not unique with this writing, but I am going to say something in perhaps a different way to help you realize the true significance of the foregoing words. You ARE the Source, Itself. You, then, create. But how do you create? and why do you create? and under what conditions do you allow Divinity to experience? If you view your life from the point of view of Divinity, the Source, what are you doing to allow the experiencing of Divinity to be Divine?

That does not mean that you have to sit in a state of worshipful meditation. What it means is that the unfoldment of your consciousness, connecting in a spiraling manner with your divinity, can be viewed objectively. If you get to that objective point of view of self, looking at your life here on the Earth from the focus of your Divinity, you will begin to attract to your life those things that are Divine. You will invoke them. It will no longer be necessary to stay in a pattern that is familiar because you do not have any reason for going beyond it.

The reason that you have remained, perhaps for aeons, in one pattern is that you could not see beyond it. Allow your Divinity to see beyond it. Allow this focus from the point of view of Divinity to guide you. If you say, now, in answer to this, "I do not understand how to do it. It does not work for me," Then I suggest you use the following direct and practical exercise to aid you in making this connection.

I want you to imagine or visualize a framework, a reference point, or truly a series of reference points by which you can view your current Earth existence. This is an exercise in seeing from the point of view of your own Divinity while you are still focused within your present physical vehicle.

It is important to actually do this exercise because although you may see what I am talking about just by reading it, you will not and cannot understand it completely until you have brought the exercise into your experience.

All right, then, sit in a straight backed chair with your feet flat on the ground, your spine erect, and your hands on your knees, palms up, and begin to imagine a framework about twelve inches above your head. It contains upright posts that are connected by means of horizontal posts - a framework. Now, with your "spiritual hands", move that framework from its current position of about twelve inches above your head, give it a push and let it go up another twelve inches. You allow the consciousness of self to have, on the physical plane, a larger framework of reference. Of course, this is symbolic, but that is the first step toward working with self, to create the framework within which you may now exist, physically. You tell self, symbolically, that the framework of your existence has been enlarged. You may, if you wish, also use your spiritual hands to push it out horizontally as well as vertically another twelve inches. This enlarges the framework of your physical existence all the way around. After doing this, meditate a few moments about the enlargement of your physical existence.

Why is it that you wish it enlarged? Does it in the enlarged portion contain now your purposes within the Cosmic Plan? I say to you, "Yes, it does." That the reason for enlarging it IS to reference this area that we may call your purposes.

Now, the following symbolic experience will aid you to begin to see what your purposes are. You have enlarged the framework of your existence and we've said to move it visually in all directions twelve inches. As you do, see this extra volume inside the framework, which is now a part of your physical, begin to vibrate and you can see the luminous quality of it. This vibration begins to permeate all of the rest of your physical existence that is framed within this outline. The magnetic attraction of it begins to raise your vibration. Let us equate it to a specific color. For the purposes of this writing, let us use the Ninth Ray - the blue with some green luminosity. See that extra volume begin to pulse as you enlarge the framework of your physical existence. And as it does, this beautiful blue-green luminosity, the ninth ray, begins to flood your physical structure. It begins to pulse with a regular beat. This regular vibration, this regular beat is the beat of the creative process, itself, which has been enlarged within you. By doing this, you can experience the enlargement of your understanding, of your physical existence. This beat of the creative process literally becomes a part of your conscious awareness. It pulses within this Ninth Ray. It is a regular beat and it tells you that you have, now, approached the understanding of your purpose in an increased manner.

Begin, then, to recognize the truth of this statement. Allow the Ninth Ray pulsing to aid you as it gathers and focuses. Allow the consciousness to come to a single point, a one-pointedness that will direct you to realize the purposes of self as a Divine being that creates for the Cosmic Plan. Allow this one-pointedness to remain. You might direct it from the third-eye area, projecting it out to all existence, but focusing it there in an integrated and focused manner.

After there has been a realization about the purposes, then begin to recognize WHO you are. How could one have Divine purposes if one were not Divine? The realization needs to be made that there is no difference between you and the Source. **You are the Source, the Source is you**. You, then, can recognize, can realize this statement is true. The following exercise, if done immediately after the foregoing will help you to realize it.

As you view from the third eye area see a large encompassing plane on your inner focus. It is white in nature and it contains everything. It is the Source, Itself. You know and recognize that it is everywhere. You can, with your inner projection, see everything there. Now, notice something interesting. You have been viewing it, projecting it through the third eye area, projecting it as a plane that exists everywhere. When you view self, now, keeping that focus, that projection, you can see, you can feel, you can hear, you can sense, you can REAL-IZE that you ARE the Source. There is no difference. The here is there, the there is here, you are a part of the all and the all is a part of you.

Now, realize this by projecting forward the Source area as you have been doing and then looking deeply within self and seeing there is no difference. The Source is the same as you are. There is no difference except perhaps that you have not realized it. Attempt, now, to move your focus to this encompassing plane and to see the Source there. Move your focus to within self and notice that you are there also. You and the Source are the same. The Source is here, the Source is there, the Source IS. You ARE. I AM.

When our perceptions become misaligned, we need to look at why this occurs. Basically, all is vibration, or as Djwhal perceives it and works with it so well, all is energy. The underlying causes of such mis-alignment are within the energy or the vibration of each of you. We look, then, at the mis-alignment of your energy with the Source, Itself - at the ways in which your vibration varies from the ideal. Now, your vibration is unique, but is meant to be completely harmonious. However, if you form mis-conceptions about your own uniqueness, or become confused about what the purpose of self is, in a sense, then, you cut off your participation within the Wholeness by sounding forth a tone that does not reflect the tone of the Source vibration. You must be completely harmonious with the Source, Itself, because you ARE the Source, Itself. If your point, your focus does not vibrate to the main and original tone that went forth as you individualized, you have become confused. You then misinterpret life as you send forth a non-compatible vibration. You need to, through clearing, learn to sound the tone that was meant for you to originally sound and each one of you has a unique tone within the Source.

In order to understand this and work with it, you must work from your present point of reference. By specifically giving you vibrational patterns, we can allow you to move beyond your present reference point. Now, you do not have to know anything about singing. You do not have to have a trained voice. You do not have to begin anywhere except right where you are.

I will seek to aid you to reflect your true tone, but you must begin right where you are. This means that by sending forth your call, you can attract the All-Knowingness in direct proportion to the harmoniousness of that tone to the Source; in direct proportion to the clarity with which your tone is sounded. Again, your clarity allows you to connect with that Divine point, that individual focus, within the All-Knowingness. When you reflect and sound forth clearly, the interchanging vibration within the Source, as far as your own point of focus is concerned, becomes the full partnership that it was meant to be.

I would like, now, to talk about this with reference to the Earth plane. You, then, are an individual focus within the whole Earth experience. Physically speaking the Earth is the Wholeness. You experience within it as part of this Wholeness. From this viewpoint you can see how much the Wholeness we call the Earth is currently learning. Upheavals are taking place - great changes. As these changes become more and more apparent, they are reflected within the physical structure of the Earth, Itself. These changes that you bring about first become a part of the spiritual body of the Earth, but as they become more and more apparent, they are reflected within the physical earth, itself. They are reflected deeply within the Earth and at times they burst forth to the surface. Now, this is a cleaning, or a cleansing process; it is necessary to clear out pressures from evolution. Some cleansing will be needed, no matter what else comes into being in man's evolutionary spiral now. By that I mean, as Djwhal has stated, humanity may avoid many of the catastrophic events which have been projected, but some are necessary from a cleansing point of view.

When one, whether an individual person or an individual planet, is evolving and learning, and becoming, there are pressure points that must be equalized, because the learning process for most is not completely balanced. It is important for you to recognize that need for balance in your own physical structure, as well as to recognize that same need in what is happening on the Earth. The earth is striving, now, valiantly to balance its growth. About the time it does that, then another cyclic event is re-stimulated and it becomes a little out of balance in another way. That's why it is so important to balance yourself as you are a miniature replica of the Wholeness that we have said is the Earth on the physical plane. By balancing your miniature replica, you allow the Wholeness to become a little more balanced and the whole evolution of the Earth to be more balanced. It is an important contribution to your planet's growth pattern.

How can this be? Well, your specific vibration sounds forth now within the Wholeness and if it is balanced, if it is stable, then its balance and its stability become a part of the Earth's evolution, of the Earth's vibration. If it is unbalanced and not stable when it sounds forth, this, too, becomes a part of the Earth's evolution and vibration. The more stable physically that humanity is, now, the more stable the physical Earth will be. This is why I am going extensively into stabilizing physical structures. Some have said they were surprised that I would be interested in helping you in this area, but the stability of the miniature replica within the Wholeness is truly the key to the evolution and stability of the Wholeness, as stated before.

If you can see that you are a reflection of the Oneness, the Oneness is a reflection of you, that there is no difference; and what you are, it is, and what you are becoming, it is becoming, then you can begin to see that you have more responsibility than you thought before, in this matter of evolution. It is easy when you look at the millions of beings on the planet - billions, truly - to become a little lost, to say, "perhaps I make no difference. I am but one among many." I, Vywamus, say to you that as you have been told, each being, each focus is dear to the Creator, is cherished by the Oneness. Each is important. Each uniqueness is brought home in the love aspect of the Creator. You are equally beloved of the Oneness. You are cherished and appreciated and loved. This means that each one's part is noticed, each one's part is the WAY that the Wholeness, the All-Knowingness partakes of existence. We all share it together. The togetherness cannot be over-emphasized.

That brings me to my next point. This next step in evolution makes us all more aware of the Oneness, of our part within it. We begin to see more and more the group approach to evolution, to living. We understand that the Allness is not a place, it is a group of focuses, and we are one. This means that, in a reflected manner here on the Earth, you all learn within a group experience. Now you do that already. You are within the World that is one group. You are within a specific hemisphere that is another group. You are within a specific continent that is another group. You are within a specific country that is another group. And you know, state, county, city, neighborhood, family, all of these units are groups.

Now, you all have experienced within groups and have formed conclusions about them. By clearing self of erroneous conclusions in the area of groups, you can move self forward in your evolution, in your understanding of the Wholeness, of the Oneness. This is a specific way to understand what IS more clearly.

Explore this area completely, remove as many blocks as you can recognize. Ask for help in this area, because it truly is a key to understanding Wholeness, to appreciating Oneness through the growth experience. Share with others, recognize that all is, that we are but a focus within the Wholeness and it is reflected everywhere back to our particular focus. See that the sharing process creates the opportunity to know we are together.

THE EARTH'S INDIVIDUALIZATION

At this critical point in history, mankind must assume responsibility for moving to the next level. He must consciously invoke the next level. This is critical, important and necessary. It depends upon the skill of humanity as to what product results. The most important skill is the perception, the overall knowing and recognizing of what is being sought. To know what is being sought, one must equate it again to the Wholeness, to the Oneness and see that the Earth's evolution is a part of a much larger plan. This overall plan which the Earth reflects is specifically moving the Earth to its point of release from a holding position, or a more resistive level of existence into what will eventually be its own spiritual state. Now, to explain that statement, let me say this. Everything is growing, becoming, and evolving. The Earth is doing this within the Wholeness. Can you conceive of the Earth, yes our Earth, reaching the point of evolvement at which it becomes completely perceptive of its own state? The Earth has not yet reached this point. It is aware of the Wholeness but it is not yet aware of its own state.

We could equate the earth's present level to the animal kingdom here on the Earth. Each animal partakes of a group consciousness. It understands the group, itself. It does not attune to individuality. It knows, yet, of the group only. Thus, it protects the herd, if you will. Now, you may say what about individual members of the animal kingdom that fight and so forth. This is but the group in its seeking to understand itself completely. Certain focuses or beings within the group individualize, but the group consciousness, itself, is not individualized.

In a Cosmic sense, on the Cosmic scale of awareness, the physical Earth now approaches the point of individualization in its consciousness. It has been aware of the Wholeness. It now is reaching for a greater understanding of self. Now, if you consider this statement, it will show you the progress of all evolution on every level as it fits together. First, Wholeness, then specific group consciousness. Within the Wholeness groups are individualized and they begin their evolution. Then within that group specific focuses are individualized.

This could be considered on many levels. And as I said earlier, our Wholeness that we consider the Source level may be but a group experience within a much more perceptive encompassing level.

The Earth, although in a sense a group consciousness, is in a larger sense an individualized portion of a group, itself. This group, of which the Earth is an individualized part, is called "physical existence " This perhaps will frame for you in a different way your understanding of the Earth and how it fits into the overall scheme of things. The Creator established physical existence as a group effort, individualized specific universes, specific galaxies, specific solar systems, specific planets, a group within a group, within a group, within a group, etc. You can take it to whatever level you wish. The microcosm and the macrocosm, you see, fit together up to the Wholeness. The point here is to see that the Earth approaches the point where it will consciously recognize self and know that it is Divine. A conscious recognition of its Divinity within the Wholeness begins after the New Age has begun.

Now, as this process begins, it will be very different here on the Earth. The Earth, itself, will take part in the New Age as never before. It will consciously participate in its growth.

Those of you who are following these words may feel that this is not what you had thought evolution to be. By that, I mean, are we not seeking from the individual state to attune to the Wholeness? Yes. You as a specific unit within the Wholeness, are. But I have been talking about the physical Earth which is not, if you will, as evolved as you are. It is on a different scale of measurement of evolution. It approaches the individualization process. Now, when one approaches the individualization process, many changes take place. The Divinity, the consciousness, becomes a direct input from the Source level. It may - and is - reflected down in various steps, in various stages, but it is no longer perceived by the individualized portion as a group consciousness. The individualized portion becomes less (for a while at least) aware of others, of its own species. Previously, there was a knowingness of the group experience, and in the case of the Earth, we would say that it now knows the whole universe. It can consciously attune to any part of this universe which is its physical group.

After the individualization process which takes place now in the coming of the New Age, the Earth will interact more closely with others that are evolving and growing as it is. At that particular time, the physical interaction will be needed for a while. The Earth will not respond automatically to the others within its physical environment. That says that after the individualization process there is perceived, for a short duration of the evolutionary spiral on the physical plane, to be a barrier between that individual consciousness and the others. Many of you are just now understanding that there is no barrier between yourself and other members of humanity. The whole point of telling you this is so that you, in your more perceptive state, can aid the Earth during this new learning opportunity. All of us that will interact with the Earth at that time can help move rapidly beyond this state, help it see beyond the short (in a sense of evolution) period in which it perceives that it is an individual but not the Wholeness as it did just shortly before. I would say that humanity owes it to the Earth to assist it as this period begins. The Earth in its individualized state will quickly respond to the pull, to the call, of a higher perception.

We will, in a Cosmic sense, and I am one that is involved in this, be working directly with the Earth's consciousness. As those of you in the Foundation are working on your blocks, we will be inputting to the Earth directly on its blocks. We will be aiding it. But if you approach the Earth and begin to interact with it, begin to build up its trust, its support, its interchange with you, now, at this time, then when the New Age begins, you will have a good rapport, a good relationship with it, then, to aid it during this critical period of its evolution.

Soon it will outgrow its temporary blind spots. It will perceive the Wholeness again, and this time Wholeness will be perceived in relation to self and the Wholeness will respond. The Earth will understand its own purposes, its own part in the cosmos, and this, of course, is the purpose of Divinity - to understand, to know, to share, to become ever more aware of Divinity and its evolution.

CHAPTER 6

CENTERING - A MEANS TO EVOLVE

As you begin to understand that you create your own life, you open up the way to see through cosmic perspectives. You will see, or view, existence more and more from these cosmic perspectives, but your ability to utilize what you have seen or gained in your understanding will come from your ability to function from a point of awareness that I call "centeredness." I suppose "balance" would be another word to use here, and certainly a valid one, but centeredness conveys the meaning of self as the Whole and certainly that is true.

To gain further insight into what I mean here, let us use the following example. Let us say in your life you have reached a point where you have many responsibilities within your personal life, but are now assuming responsibilities within the wider perspective of aiding others, aiding the Earth and aiding the Cosmic Plan. How, then, can you remain centered - balanced, if you will - when coming at you from every "direction" or aspect are these responsibilities? Each one requires energy, time and your sense of purpose, your Divine beingness responds to the needs in each of these areas.

Each time you arise from the sleep state, welcome your new day, your new opportunity to center your efforts, to see more clearly beyond what the previous day has shown you. The reason for sequential time, dear one, is to allow the learning of self to literally be "tracked," meaning you can look at self as it was perceived a year ago, look at self now, and see sequentially the fuller, more complete understanding that you now have. Some of you may say here "I can't see anything." But, if you are truly honest with self, if you look deeply, you will see that you are gaining understanding beyond previous perspectives.

Trust is a connector, a means to allow something that you have not yet seen or understood to begin. I suggest to you, then, that each time you arise, each morning, you trust the Divine part of self, you literally say to your higher self, "I trust you and because I do, I can center myself within all of what is coming to me and know that each experience that I connect with will simply be a supportive focus, a supportive mechanism for my learning, for my self-discovery process." Trust, then, can be viewed as having a particular energy composition. You can literally put it on as a garment and wear it in your life. I assure you that trusting the Divine, the creative potential, will pay rich dividends.

You may, perhaps, wish to clear the area of trust from a subconscious point of view. All of you in trusting the Divine, have some responses, some beliefs which may make trusting difficult. For some of you this is an important area to clear, for others it will simply enlarge the way you are already able to trust. Whichever is true in your case, working within the belief structure in the trust area will pay many dividends to you personally as you seek to remain centered in your life.

Recognize, then, that true centeredness is the acceptance of self as a Divine being who is part of the interaction of the Whole, meaning that centeredness allows you to recognize your relationship within the Whole. It is an indicator of such a relationship. Thus, centering self will invoke the more ideal usage of your relationships with humanity, the animal kingdom, etc. within the Whole.

Consider that previous statement, dear one. It is important. When you are centered you are more open, more relaxed, more receptive. You may not be, at that moment, any clearer, but you are more open and, when more open to accepting of relationships within the Whole, all of your responsibilities on every level can interact with you, can be related to easier, more completely and more joyfully.

Your responsibilities, or your conscious evolvement within the Whole will always be increasing as you see self's centering as possible, as you more and more allow it. What will come forth, then, is the ability to handle, to experience whatever life brings to you in a manner that does not overwhelm, does not confuse, but stretches you beyond what you have been. Centering, then, is a means to allow existence and life itself to interact with you in a more cosmic manner.

CHAPTER 7

WHAT IS LOVE?

Love, my friends, is the ability to understand clearly from every point of view and to appreciate every point of view. It becomes necessary to experience encompassing Love in order to understand, in totality, what the Allness, the Oneness is, and its purposes. If you can see this, then the next question, of course, is "How do I learn to know Love more and more completely? How do I understand? I find that I think I know about Love, but encompassing Love? I'm not sure what that means."

I say to you now, this is the journey, this is the Quest. And for most upon the Earth, they see it as a reflection, as a statement. The search for Love on the physical level, then, becomes involved with others. We seek it through others. Now, if you can understand that love through others is a reflection, then you have taken one step further in your understanding. It does not negate seeking the reflection, but perhaps you will wish to seek the direct experience also.

Encompassing Love means understanding Love everywhere, seeing it from every point of view, seeing it from every angle and knowing that it is the key, the focus upon which all existence moves. It, in a sense, is the lubricant upon which existence depends. Now if you consider that statement, it really does say a great deal. Without the lubricant of Love, an event that is unfolding is irritating, the parts that come together grind instead of flow. There is no way to blend together all of the parts that make up wholeness on whatever level without this Love lubricant. Now some of you are just beginning to see that Love really is nothing personal. It has far-stretching and far-reaching possibilities. You are beginning to glimpse the encompassing stretch or enfoldment of Love. I like to say it this way, "As the Source Light considered and reflected, Love was very active, and thus it built all of existence within a Love framework. There was so much that it could stretch everywhere. It was used as a lubricant. It was used as a bridge. It was used as a framework. There was ample Love. It could be used ever more completely and was and is and will be. Thus we see Love and its encompassing possibilities stretch everywhere.

Now each of you have but to realize this is true to tap in on those unlimited possibilities, potentialities within self, the Love that is sprinkled so liberally everywhere is there when you can perceive it. You have but to reach out for it. You have but to allow its presence. It will enfold you. It will hold you. It will nurture you. What are we saying then? We are saying that the Allness, the Oneness, has an aspect that is very expansive, never limiting, all encompassing and that aspect, my friends, is Love. Think of Love. What is it? Begin to analyze, to reflect, to attune to Love. All of it, not just your current understanding of it.

A good exercise is: before you go to bed, place the word Love where you will see it as you awaken. Place it on the outside where you can see it. And then as you arise, place it on the inside where you can use it. Involve yourself totally for one day in Love. Use it as a reference point from which to view everything. Attempt to nurture all that you meet. It does not mean that you necessarily have to DO anything. It just means that you will be Love. Others may partake of it or not as they choose, but when you approach everyone with Love as Love, you begin to emulate the great one that you call the Christ, the great one that walked among you. He was Love. He is Love. He will be Love. Love is present in you as it is in Him. Become Love. View life through it.

Now, for some of you, as you attempt to do this, there may be some resistance. But when you look at this resistance, you will see that it is but a momentary misunderstanding that can easily be removed through your clearing process, a momentary misunderstanding in the Cosmic sense. You too, each one of you, are Love. Each is the part of Divinity that is to spread Love by manifesting it, by utilizing it.

How is Love manifested in an encompassing way? First, by seeing others through Love. I have learned a little about how to do this and as I view each of you, I can see your point of evolution, but what I also see is your Love, your beauty, your unique participation in the Wholeness. And I appreciate it. I do not dwell on those areas that you do not yet un-

79

derstand, except as a teacher to aid you. But when I am looking at you, I appreciate you and Love and cherish you. You mean much to me, as I view you through Love. I would not give up any of you and I do not have to. We are together and we can Love and cherish each unique interpretation of Love.

Stimulate your Love aspect when you are seeking something to meditate on. Consider Love. It is a vast subject and you will never run out of areas within it to contemplate. Consider it through the senses when you fill your cup of love so that it feels as if it will run over, but it cannot. It is ever enlarging. Then, consider, how do you feel it? Do you smell it? Do you see it? Do you hear it? All of these senses, the entire feeling nature, is especially important with Love. Get in touch with it. Know not only the physical response to the Love aspect but also the response which occurs on all other levels of self. You can learn, then, to align all parts of self through Love.

If you will do the following exercise, you will accomplish several things at once. You will help to spread Love throughout your physical world. You will help spread love through out every other level also. In a personal sense you will stretch the amount of Love you can hold. You will grow because of working with Love. You will also aid to balance the four bodies. Each one responds to Love. And if you use Love as a focus, each one comes when you call it into perfect alignment. Does this say, my friends, and I truly believe it does, that when you remain filled with Love, when this Love is forever full, all of self is completely balanced and you serve to ever increase the Love aspect of the Source Light, Itself? Yes, I think we have hit upon a truth here. Each one of you by understanding what Love is, by attuning to it, by becoming Love will aid the Source and through that, self.

Now, spiritual teachers have been saying this for aeons. Be Love. Understand Love. And some have tried and succeeded. But most here on your planet have not yet done so. Why is that? Well, perhaps we could say that encompassing Love and experiencing it is a journey to the very center, to the very core of self. Now, perhaps some of you are not yet aware that this is true. But if there is resistance to looking at Love, to being Love, to sharing it in an encompassing way, then look at this possibility. Does becoming Love make you feel vulnerable? Does it? Does it allow others to see what you really are? If you feel this way, you probably will want to look at this area and clear it. If you become Love and others do not, does it perhaps, separate you from those that you have known? It does not, truly. But if you believe this is true, then perhaps you should look at this in your clearing system, also. If you will persist in these exercises that I give you here in this discussion, they will aid you.

And so I say to you, examine Love, through your meditations and within your own beliefs. Look at it, become aware of it. See how encompassing it truly is. If you cannot really attune to it as you would like, keep practicing, because practicing with Love in the highest, most encompassing sense of what is necessary to reach the goal of understanding will aid the Source Light. The Source will expand through you to greater understanding of the Wholeness as far as the Love aspect is concerned. Is this not an exciting goal?

For some of you who are looking for your purposes, I assure you this is a part of them. And if you are looking at your purposes area and your knowingness says, "Yes, this is a part of my purposes," know that I, Vywamus, say to you, "This is a part of your purposes. You can begin right now today as you read this book." How exciting! How purposeful! Each one of you has many purposes. You have them in an ever more expanded way as you understand them ever more expansively. Begin, then, with Love. Consider it. Know that it is on several levels. One of the most familiar levels is that of personal Love, which needs to be shared to support self; personal love requires that someone return it to support you. On the next level, love is more encompassing and you give it without requiring that it be returned, but if it is returned, you appreciate it, you like it and perhaps you really look for it. On the next level, love is still more encompassing and you give it in an unrestrained manner to those around you and to the planet Itself. This Love is completely allowing and knows that it is going forth into everything and may not necessarily be returned through some one else and it is not necessary that it so be. This Love contains what one might call compassion for others' position without any judgment of it; it is completely accepting of others as they are.

The next step up that can now be understood by humanity on the physical plane, is a point where you are Love incarnate. You are Love. And all of the Love that is reflects through you, becomes magnified and enhanced through being a part of you. You send it forth and you receive it. You act as a receiver and a transmitter. You are Love. This is your goal here on the physical plane. An example of this was the Christ. He walked your Earth as Love. He showed you the way. He said, "I am the way," and of course, this is true. The "I Am" is the way. He gave a magnificent example to others of a physical being who showed that Love could walk on the Earth. You are Love.

The example has been set. Follow it. You have but to walk in the footsteps that have already been set upon your planet. I say to you, cultivate an awareness of Love and become It as you are able to realize more and more what it is.

CHAPTER 8

SHARING, WHAT DOES THIS MEAN?

As you seek to understand, to learn, you become aware that learning can be shared. However, for a long period before that, learning seems very personal and something that is yours, nothing gets through to self but the personal part of learning. To give you an example, a small child discovers all about the physical body. This is a personal exploration, however, and the child feels a sense of ownership in regard to the physical structure. His/her physical body, then, seems a personal learning tool and truly has nothing to do with anyone else. As the child grows, he/she begins to see that others also have physical bodies and begins to appreciate beauty within physical bodies which are viewed. Truly, there is much beauty within a physical body. I, Vywamus, view them with a sense of wonder, seeing the symmetry and flow of the design, the flow of the structure. I view your physical bodies with great appreciation. At the point where one begins to see beyond his/her own body, begins to look at the bodies of others, an opportunity exists to relate emotionally.

If you are emotionally expressive, meaning that you acknowledge emotional responses within self and allow them to be expressed freely and easily rather than restricting them, you will become aware of the emotions of others and these emotional responses which are then shared with others are part of the sharing process that I am discussing here. Certainly, we may discuss sharing in a number of ways and I intend to do so, but being willing to share with others emotionally is important. Those of you who are able to express your feelings, able to show them to others, able to allow them to be visible within self can be the ones who exemplify the Source's exuberance, joy, sense of humor, unconditional love, humility and appreciation.

Of course, it is important to recognize that when emotionally expressive, perhaps those emotions called pain, trauma, sorrow, loss, etc. are not necessary; they are connected to misperceptions and one seeks to release these misperceptions within self. We, the teachers, have talked over and over again about the need to analyze, about the need to be conceptual, but there is also the need to express one self emotionally. This gets into the sharing/caring focus that you are seeking to manifest as a part of your Divine potentiality.

Your beautiful Djwhal Khul is an excellent example of someone who utilizes the emotional body in a productive and extremely helpful manner. All of you have felt his enthusiasm, his joy, his appreciation, his love. Because of the vast store of appreciation that comes through him to the Earth, the students who work with him often treasure and appreciate the connection with him, and also learn and release deep blocked areas within self. I guess you could say that I, Vywamus, am a "fan" of Djwhal's, one of his greatest admirers. One reason I admire him so much is his especially proficient use of the emotional response.

As you come together, all of you on the Earth, you share your environment, you share with each other this spiritual opportunity that has become a physical focus. Basically, then, you all care about one another. This is part of your Divine heritage, the caring nature. Sometimes, misperceptions about the caring nature of self and of its usage keep you from being able to express it deeply and fully, but it is there, a component of self that is a Source-level quality of self.

The Source expresses through all of us, and one Divine mystery is the Source's ability to love, understand and CARE for each of us in an equal and loving manner. The Source shares its love and caring. It has an unlimited amount of it, enough to go around, enough to share with everyone. You, too, as a Divine Being, have enough love, enough caring to share with everyone. Don't you? I am here to tell you that you do, and your recognition of the learning and discovery process using the heart center or heart chakra area is, perhaps, a major part of your evolutionary process.

You share your planet. You may feel you have no choice, that you came into a physical structure and here you are and here everyone else is and, thus, you're rather "stuck" with the circumstances. This area, then, of being willing to share is important. Certainly, as I have said over and over again, the realization process is absolutely essential to aid you in your self-discovery process. It is necessary to release blocks, make realizations, but, at the same time, from another point of view, wherever you are within your transformational process, you must be willing to share with others, and work toward expressing your true caring nature.

As you evolve and grow, life will present an unlimited number of opportunities to share your discoveries with others, but perhaps even more importantly, to share who you are and your caring nature with others. Each one of us, truly, is a pillar of light, a supportive pillar, if you will, within the Whole. Sometimes when a "little lamb" is lost and cries, if you are the one the little lamb turns to in its lost state, be willing to share a little of your strength, your light, your caring nature. Each time you do, it gets easier to continue to utilize your caring nature.

You see, these gifts, these tools of the Divine, are there for all of us to use, but we must be willing to familiarize ourselves with how to use them and then we can share them with everyone else. Thus does the Whole grow, learn and evolve. I say to you now: sharing will bring to you all of your potential because you will invoke through your sharing, caring nature responses from others that teach you, that will allow you to see what is available to you as a Divine being now. If you take one little step and share with another briefly, you have "lit up" the evolution of the Whole in a very cosmic manner indeed!

Dear ones, as you share, you attract the attention of Sourceness, whether we call it Self or the Whole. You become a magnet that attracts a clearer, more evolved manifestation of Sourceness.

CHAPTER 9

THE BRIDGING PROCESS

Love builds a bridge of understanding, of awareness, which connects you to your ability to utilize all of your strengths and abilities in your life. We have been discussing Love in various ways, but to see it as an actual energy which structures for you, or bridges for you, to a point of clearer understanding is important.

Now you may say, "Vywamus, I don't understand. Love is important. I can feel that. But how can it bridge, now?" I say to you that Love not only bridges, it creates openings, and the most important opening is to your own evolution. The key or means to utilizing your own abilities is in the Love and allowingness area. Many of you are quite "hard" on yourself, feeling perhaps not fully adequate to use all of your potential. The bridge to these potentialities is structured through the love and allowingness area. Through your desire to be an unconditional expression of love in order to aid others, this allowingness area can be stimulated.

If you desire to aid others but are frustrated at times because you don't know what to say to a particular individual, I would suggest the following: first of all, seek to see them unconditionally through love. This can "relax" you or allow you to view the other persons without judging them. Many times words flow on unconditional love in a manner that is not possible otherwise. You may, through your love, surprise yourself at the words which come forth, because you have not brought them forth mentally, but through your love. Allow that and see from it that a bridge has been built to aid another.

Don't forget also to flow the love to self as a Divine being with unlimited potential. View self as a divine being whom you are seeking to aid as you would with another. Let the love and allowingness area bridge for you the process of learning and discovery which is called evolution.

Remember, a bridge connects, and what you are seeking to connect is the learning process, all perspectives or points of view that you have gathered together into the cosmic or unlimited point of view which you seek to enter now. Recognize this bridge which flows love forth and brings back to you that unlimited perspective you are seeking.

CHAPTER 10

THE COMFORT FACTOR

You may think that my association with you puts too much pressure on you to evolve. I do not mean for it to be "strenuous" but the importance of the times has me very focused into all of your potentialities. I perhaps can see them more clearly than you. I can surely aid you to realize and allow these potentialities to manifest upon the Earth plane. You are the workers who will bring forth the New Age and I, for one, intend to focus in on the ways in which to do this more and more intensely. I do not mean to insinuate that I will force anyone to do anything, but my association with each of you will be focused on helping you realize your true self, your true nature, your own unique Divinity, your own place within the Wholeness. First, however, we must break through the barriers for some of you. First, you must begin to realize what is offered here. I come now and I say to you, "Come forth into that new self; leave the shell of misconception; leave the shell that we call the 'personality'. Gather up and go forth into the new pattern that awaits you - the level of the soul. The Earth experience is a wonderful opportunity for doing this."

Now, you must realize, individually, the reasons why the misconceptions hold you, why the illusion is retained. It seems to me that for many of you there is a comfort factor involved here. The familiar is here. Thus even though you seek your Divinity, you want to do it in the framework of your present comfort. There is fear to go beyond this. However, the Earth that awaits you after the New Age will be a whole new experience and some of what you are familiar with now will be gone. Release this comfort factor now. Be willing to go beyond it. Say, "I will now institute a plan, a regimen of discipline for self, that will allow me to be ready for these changes - this cleansing time that is soon upon us." If you retain the necessity for the comfort factor, it will be a shock when the Earth no longer contains it. It will be a shock when you no longer have it. You become ready by letting go of the need for all of these things.

Now I say this carefully, knowing that you are entitled to everything that is here. You are entitled to your comfort factor as its exists. But, because you have chosen to go beyond the Earth as it is now, you must let go of this comfort factor now, also. It seems to me as I view humanity and particularly the workers, that this one aspect is what must be overcome, that truly by your dedication to service, that truly by your wish to go beyond your present position in evolution, you must let go of the need to always be comfortable, because evolution must be experienced at every level within self. If you hold on to the need to do it comfortably, that need, in a sense, keeps you from doing so in a completely enlarged and productive manner.

If your need for sleep keeps you in that bed for many, many hours a night, then look at that. Can you perhaps get by with less sleep? Why would you do that? It would be, my friends, because you have chosen to serve. It would be because you see beyond this present place. It would be because you see the needs of others. It would be, my friends, because you wish, now to experience at a higher level, letting go of your needs, wants and desires at every opportunity. Choose to go forth. Choose to allow self to align with service in an ever more encompassing way.

Now I am not saying here that you should go into an ashram experience and let go of your family obligations. I am saying that in your personal life a little more discipline for many of you will pay rich dividends. If you choose to experience more (and my example was "sleep") instead, you will of course work on the inner level. This is valuable. But your attention now, my friends, needs to be on the Earth plane - on the outer experience. The more time you are here the better. This does not mean that the physical structure doesn't need rest; it does. But you can get by, in a sense, with less sleep, and it will be because you have chosen to do so. You may stay at any one point in your evolution for as long as you wish. But, if you choose now to serve, if you choose now to unlock within self all of what has been, to move self to a more perceptive level, then this is a key to it - giving up those things that seem compulsive - such as moving beyond the need to sleep long hours. It doesn't mean that you can do it in five minutes. It means that you can begin to work on it. You can consciously choose to change the present pattern. You can take out the compulsiveness from within self and then with your conscious choice, you can begin to go beyond your present level. Your dedication to service will accomplish it. Your dedication to the Cosmic Plan will bring it about.

Now, your contact with me will be rather intense, because I will give you those teachings that will move you rapidly to the soul-merged state if you will do them. But you consciously choose now whether you discipline self enough to accomplish them. I am not what you would call as diplomatic as Djwhal Kuhl. I do give you what you need. It is your choice whether or not you accept my words and implement them. But I will be giving you much material, many ways to see beyond the "now" of the Earth plane experience. I say to you, my friends, "RESPOND TO THE CALL OF YOUR SOUL. COME FORTH NOW TO ITS CALL. IT CALLS YOU. DIVINITY BECKONS AND I SEE YOU EX-PAND. I, VYWAMUS, WILL AID YOU." Divinity, as never before, gathers here perceptively on the Earth and each one of you has the opportunity to respond to it.

You will hear me toning much. You will hear me aiding the Divinity within you through vibrating certain tones. They are set specifically at a vibration-al level to open the door within you. But you must go through that door, and self discipline is needed to do so. Now, if you look at it from an analytical viewpoint, you can see how disciplined the Source is. The Source has a goal and creation moves per-fectly towards that goal. Creation keeps expanding in a focused, in a disciplined manner. There are never any detours. There are never times when the

Source says, "I am too tired to respond. I need more rest. I need more sleep." Discipline sets the tone for your evolution. You do not feel martyred. It is done eagerly, it is done gladly. It is done because you are emulating the Source Itself. You know that the way to serve is by a constant conscious application of your perception.

Please do not misunderstand. You are human beings and thus need respite from some of this intensity. You need friends and social occasions. You need times of complete rest. This is a part of physical life. But each of you, my friends, are disciples. Some of you are getting close to what Djwhal calls the "initiate" state and you must realize that service, that the Creator's Cosmic Plan is your all and you must begin to make it your all. You must, then, completely integrate each experience into your life. You must not just assume that the service area will take care of itself. You must bring it forth by your discipline and by the way that you live. You must as one that is initiating the creative process, bring it forth. That is what the "initiate" state means. The means to begin. You have begun to work up to the point of 100% service for the Creator. That is the esoteric meaning of the word. It is the beginning of the dedicated state beyond which the expanded service is greater than any of you can know.

Now, I do not wish to overwhelm any of you. Djwhal Kuhl will lead you step-by-step to this initiate state which is the soul-merge. But I, Vywamus, will help you to understand that ALL is awaiting you after you initiate by your discipline, by your willingness to serve this great event that we call "TOTAL SERVICE TO THE CREATOR'S COSMIC PLAN." Your responsibility is to bring self to that point after which the Divinity within self will direct, will initiate all that follows.

I, Vywamus, say to you, "AID SELF NOW. RESPOND TO THE CALL OF YOUR SOUL."

CHAPTER 11

SEEING OPPORTUNITIES NOW

Begin now to see more clearly. When I make this statement, I want to explain it so that all will understand what is meant. CLARITY IS THE ABILITY TO SEE WITHOUT REFERENCING THE PAST, WITHOUT LOOKING AT WHAT HAS OCCURRED. Clarity is seeing an opportunity objectively. It is the way that the Source Light views existence - with clarity. It sees all possibilities in existence, and it begins to explore them in a comprehensive manner. Truly, existence has been called "complicated" but it is not. It is just the result of the Source Light exploring every facet possible in the experiencing mode. When you can understand that completely, it comes through in a multi-dimensional way. To put this in perspective, if we had a cube that we could call existence, one dot of existence would be your present totality, and the rest of the cube is made up by other dots which are totalities within the Wholeness we are referencing as a cube. Or consider a sphere that has as many facets as you can imagine, and then some. It has the potential for an unlimited number of facets. Each facet is a totality, is an existence that is focused by one particular point that we reference with the Source Light. You can be a productive part of this

Wholeness by clearly seeing what existence truly is and bringing forth all of your potentialities.

The physical plane gives you almost unlimited opportunities to reference your potentialities directly as you experience here, now, on the Earth. However, you must recognize these opportunities when they come to you. You must choose to utilize them. You must be aware enough to see how this particular opportunity will allow you to reference your potentialities. The Source Light that you are experiences and learns by its experiencing mode. You, too, can learn from everything.

Have you, for example, had an opportunity to experience with new people and said,"I am too tired, I will not do that now." This, in my perception, is a missed opportunity. You have missed a way of exchanging, of communicating with other parts of the Wholeness. I am not saying that every time you are invited somewhere you should just automatically go. Of course not. I am saying if an opportunity is presented to you that you should recognize it as that - an opportunity to learn by experiencing -and then you should take advantage of it, not just be comfortable where you are, too tired, perhaps, or too uninterested to make the effort to go beyond the familiar pattern. The reason why I spoke of an interchange with new people is because new perceptions, when interchanged with your perceptions, allow you to learn, allow you to grow, allow you to perceive in a different way from what you had previously understood. This is enlarging when you allow it to do so, when you know that this is an opportunity to learn.

One such as Djwhal Khul learns from every opportunity, knows that he can learn from an exchange with each of you. He told me he has learned more in this two-year period talking to all of you than perhaps he did in many lifetimes on the Earth. Why is that? Because he is now more aware. He recognizes that interchange, discussions with different perceptions, can be used as a learning tool. You see, the teacher learns more than the student. It is so interesting to him to see and learn through his exchange with you. You, also, when you can objectively and with awareness view your interaction with everything in this manner, can learn from each and every moment of your Earth experience.

As you begin to view life on the Earth in this way, what happens? Your joy aspect awakens. It says, "Yes, the purpose of existence is to learn, and I have become aware of doing it now, all of the time. The opportunity is here all of the time and I enjoy it. I must celebrate this opportunity now by expressing joy. Gone is the pain, gone is the loss, gone is the emotional reaction that held me here in the past. What I have is Joy because I recognize that this opportunity has been given to me by the Source Light, Itself. It has allowed me now to come into physical existence." The opportunity is here to interact more and more with others who are here now, too, to communicate my perception to them, and to receive from them their perception, to learn, to grow, to evolve, to serve, my friends, to SERVE the Source Light.

Do you not see what an opportunity Earth living is? That there are many who wish it? It is not possible for all who wish it to experience it. This beautiful gem that you call "the Earth" shines, it attracts many. Far from my considering it a small dark planet as many have said that it is, it is a gem, a jewel within the Wholeness that is to be explored, is to be lived, is to be cherished, is to be LOVED, is to be experienced with the Divine knowingness of what has been offered. The Source Light brings forth a part of self and says, "Experience now, and part of that experience will be a brief span in sequential time that is called 'Earth Living' " . What joy, what gratitude, what love, what an interchange possibility this is. Now, some of you may say,"I've heard this all my life - appreciate the Earth, but I live in such pain. I live now not as I want but as I have to. I can't get beyond my pain, my stuckness, although I've tried and I am trying, I do not know how."

Well, my friends, I say to you, the opportunity is here. The Earth's evolution brings it to you right now. Here is the opportunity, and I, Vywamus, present it to you now. Know who you are. Become aware of it. Get involved with the techniques that may clear you at this time. Take the full responsibility for doing so. You are not FATED to experience anything. You are Divine, you have a choice, now. You have chosen already to partake of the Cosmic Plan for Earth. Now, do it in a larger, a more expanded manner. Attune to me now and say,"I wish to serve. Will you aid me? Come to me now, my friends, and I WILL aid you. I promise you that I, Vywamus, come now. You have invoked my presence, you have invoked my aid. We are not separate, we are one. We are but individual focuses within the Wholeness. Gather up all of your potentialities and move the Earth forward. Get involved in a group effort. Get involved in a vehicle, a service vehicle such as the Foundation or another that is seeking to aid man's evolution. Get involved and together humanity will be increasingly aware of this marvelous opportunity that comes now.

CHAPTER 12

A GENTLE 'NUDGE'

Life "nudges" one a little, from time to time. You may have noticed that. But, what truly does this statement mean? I would like to discuss this with you now in rather a comprehensive manner, so that you may see then that "nudging" is your igniting or creative sparking process. That may be an esoteric statement, but it is, dear ones, an esoteric process that we are discussing. The creative process goes beyond physical existence. It is a process that sorts out, literally sifts through everything and integrates it again to allow a more profound, more comprehensive, more exciting state to be realized.

To sort out and understand this area, then, let us look at the following situation. Let us say you are an actress/actor. You prepared yourself by getting some training in that area, let us say you attended an acting school. You graduated and began your acting career. You were given certain opportunities, certain doors were opened to you because your school recommended you, your training literally opened certain doors for you. You still had to utilize the opportunity given. Perhaps, as an example, the school recommended you to certain producers who interviewed you to see if you were suitable for a particular role. Let us say that you did well, you received several small roles and performed well. Your competency in performing was then proven. From this beginning, came forth more opportunities, larger roles. You became known as a proficient actress/actor and played several roles and played them well.

Now, let us say that ten years have passed and then your agent sends you a manuscript saying there is a part in it for you. As you read it you become very excited, your intuition tells you that this is an important opportunity for you. You accept the role eagerly, begin rehearsals and, sure enough, when the production is completed, you have gained a certain amount of fame as an actress/actor.

At this point life begins to "nudge" you a little. What does that mean? As you become visible in the creative process, certain responsibilities come forth. You may be asked to appear at benefits, you may be asked to go on tour and promote certain activities. Many doors open as life "nudges" you a little in the creative process.

In a sense you are all actors, are you not? YOU may not consider it your career, but you are on the physical level acting out a certain role, seeking to fulfill whatever requirements you believe it contains. Now, as you become more and more proficient at the "acting", life begins to "nudge" you a little. You find your responsibilities are stepped up and each time you become aware of fulfilling your role more completely there is a "nudge" which is literally a contact with the next level or next possibility that then allows the greater and perhaps, from one point of view anyway, more desirable life that you are seeking to manifest now.

Some of you, then, may wish to clear your misperceptions about the area of responsibility. Seeing what responsibility is more completely will aid you to accept those little "nudges" as they come forth. Responsibility is simply what you have accepted as the appropriate guidance system in your life, in your evolution. There is no need to either fear or resist responsibility, no need to be overwhelmed or in awe of accepting more of it. But, perhaps, from past experiences, some responses come forth that need to be cleared.

Many of you have beliefs which say, "The more responsible I am, the more I must do." Now, that seems true as far as it goes, but the next statement says, "And I will not be able to keep up with all of these responsibilities. They tend to overwhelm me." How about changing that to read: "I look forward to those areas I am responsible for. I know, I can sense the opportunity that awaits me there!" Can you see what a difference this makes? Clearing the area of responsibility, then, will allow you to accept that little "nudge" that is the Whole's evolution and which affects you because your are a part of the Whole.

As a member of the human kingdom, you share humanity's learning, humanity's discovery process. If it seems humanity demands too much of you, then again this area needs clearing. Humanity simply reflects the Whole for you. Your beliefs about the Whole come forth as you interact with humanity. Humanity will not overwhelm or cause a sense of frustration, a sense of bewilderment, a sense of confusion when you can accept and see that humanity is composed of individual Divine beings just like you, who are seeking to understand and who appreciate efforts - be they efforts of those who are on the physical level or efforts of those of us on the spiritual level - to help them recognize that the magnificent Whole is visible, responsive and clearly supportive. I say to each of you, then, a "nudge" is the Whole as it seeks to hurry you along, a little, on your path of conscious recognition of what your opportunities really are. The Source, Itself, as your Father, guides you. Use this sense of being guided to allow the unfoldment of self eternally now.

CHAPTER 13

EMERGING INTO THE LIGHT

You have been told that you are light, and indeed you are. However, it is perhaps necessary to see that light is always active, always integrating, indeed, always becoming. Light is the tool by which one sees in the fullest sense. It defines life for us if we let it.

You here now on the Earth are utilizing the light of the Earth and of humanity to learn and to grow because, as I stated before, light is an active process which is stimulated through interaction. Light then identifies spiritual growth and allows a fuller interaction with us, the spiritual teachers. The Earth and you upon it now are lighter than before, thus, we on the spiritual level see the Earth's light shining more brightly. It has become a beacon and many of us on the spiritual plane have been called by that light beacon at this time. In other writings, I discussed magnetism, and the purpose here is not to give you a conceptual, deeply technical lesson on magnetism, but let us say that the earth through its light perspective is becoming magnetic and thus draws to itself the means to grow, to evolve, to learn. We, the spiritual teachers, are what the earth draws to it now, magnetically. Through those of you who are emerging into the light of a clearer understanding, we are able to aid the earth's living process now.

It is true that life on the earth is now being lived in what has been called the "fast lane." In a vibrational sense, your earth, your world, is vibrating at a frequency that has literally picked up the pace of living on it. The earth then is lighter, but its lighter perspective is quickening the pace and I know many of you recognize that this is true. The light on your planet can be seen cosmically as I stated earlier, and of course, I am not saying that only the earth is lightening and growing, but it is at an important point on its path of evolution which is discernible to those who understand the process and know how to view it. Specific indicators that we've seen include the growing interest in understanding self. Not everyone, of course, becomes metaphysical through a search to discover self, but the process of searching deepens the discovery process of the whole planet, no matter what area specifically it is focused in. One must literally, then, see that your planet is a whole perspective and the discovery process will light it up from every point of view. Recognize that it broadens the basic understanding on your planet when many points of view learn and grow together. Your planet emerges into its full light potential through the allowingness of each person and through the communicative link of each person with others - sharing, caring, allowing, trusting - all of these are part of the emerging into the light process. Know that the radiance and beauty of your planet earth is increasing and being aided by your self- discovery process, your desire to know, to grow, to accept responsibility, to aid specific efforts or groups which present for humanity learning opportunities is important. Remember you are a member of humanity and through your joint efforts together will you allow humanity and the earth to create that beautiful light planet which will emerge from what has been. Remember even if present conditions may seem difficult, one can release difficulty by utilizing light, the active state of light, and its interaction will allow full emerging of the earth into its light potentiality. Indeed your earth is bright and its brightness is awakening all of you cosmically.

CHAPTER 14

POINTS OF VIEW ON THE EARTH NOW

Your earth, as stated in the last section, is at a very important point in its evolution. There is a letting go process which is important. In another book which is soon to be published, I, Vywamus, discuss the evolution of the earth through the four kingdoms. It is rather an interesting point of view. Your earth has four bodies or kingdoms, the mineral, plant, animal and human kingdom and it also has what Djwhal Kuhl has called the kingdom of souls, the Spiritual Hierarchy or the group of those who guide your planet from the spiritual level. This kingdom of souls is of course becoming more closely identified with the physical plane as many of you merge with your soul and evolve to a point of completion on the physical plane. Those of you who are at this point begin to aid us, to become our partners in the process of aiding humanity and its evolution.

At this time, then, many points of view are being blended on your earth, and I am speaking now beyond humanity, although, of course, within humanity this is true also. The mineral kingdom, literally the earth's physical perspective, is undergoing some extensive changes now. Psychics have seen this period as catastrophic/difficult. It need not be, but there no question, no doubt, but what it is an adjustment period for the mineral kingdom.

Stability comes through understanding, and the mineral kingdom seeks to blend all perspectives of itself to create greater understanding within itself, just as you, in your physical body, seek to have your glandular system, for example, balanced, or any other physical system balanced, so the earth seeks to balance its aspects now.

Many of you are attracted to crystals and gems. They present a point of view, or perspective, of the mineral kingdom, and each one, through its association with you, can aid the mineral kingdom to emerge, beyond any divisive points of view, or those areas that seek literally to pull it apart catastrophically.

Enjoy your friends, the crystals and the gems. Your association is important for the learning and growing of all kingdoms on the earth. I am not going to spend much time here on crystals and gems, and unless it is your wish, you need not spend hours and hours studying them either, but accept the mineral kingdom of which the crystals and gems are but an example, as your friend, and interact or communicate with it daily. Each time you do so, each time you accept the mineral kingdom, beyond just "walking on it", when you accept it as your equal, when you accept it in love, when you support it in its growth and evolution, then it can do the same for you and for all of humanity. Remember, as we stated in the previous section, light is created through interaction, through communication, and your willingness to communicate with the mineral kingdom will pay great dividends.

The plant kingdom, on the earth, is very wise. It has wisdom beyond its "years", and because of this wisdom, it literally aids the earth through being willing to participate in the evolution of your planet. One has but to look at the beauty and practicality of the plant kingdom to recognize the stability factor it provides here on your earth. Although you may not realize it, your plant kingdom earned its "freedom." It has graduated. But because of its great love and support of the earth, many dominant species of the plant kingdom have remained present, physically. It is, of course, through love that they do so. The next time you view a redwood tree, know this Divine grandeur has been a beacon of light and of great beauty on your earth for aeons. It is getting ready, finally, to leave the earth. I do not disclose the timing of this event, but it is close in a cosmic sense. Certain species of the plant kingdom have been allowed to leave the physical earth, while the kingdom in general continued to aid the evolution of the planet. Some of them have remained available on the astral level, after leaving as well.

The animal kingdom is important at this time and it is evolving well. There are certain species which are now "phasing out." This does not mean you have lost anything on the earth, but when a species dies out, it means it has evolved beyond its present physical vehicle or structure. Learn to let go of the species. Allow evolution to work through the animal kingdom.

This does not mean that humanity cannot foster or assist a species when it has few in number - in point of fact, many times that species is working on survival and has earned the assistance. But sometimes when, in a sudden, seemingly unexpected manner, all members of a species are wiped out, this is not accidental, but a part of the evolution of your animal kingdom.

Your animal kingdom seeks to identify themselves through a group process as independent and yet useful to the group. Humanity could learn a great deal about groups from the animal kingdom, and I would encourage those of you who are working within a group to learn from the animal kingdom's knowledge in this area.

Humanity is the next kingdom and we have discussed it in many ways already, but I wish to point out that evolution results from blending or integrating the mineral, plant, animal, human and teacher levels. As a member of humanity, you perhaps, more than any other kingdom, have the ability to actively affect every other kingdom. Your decisions are important, your interaction and communication vital - both with each other and with the other kingdoms. You are in a very real sense the pivotal point of the planet's evolution. Note I did not say the most important point, but the pivotal one, the one that through allowingness, communication, love, trust, and sharing, can bring forth the desired state of life, or quality of life each of you seeks here on the earth now. This is very real. This esoteric discussion applies to you now in your life. Recognize, or seek to, that each decision you make, each step you take, each effort you make, affects the coming together of all points of view on your earth, which is called evolution.

CHAPTER 15

STIMULATING GROWTH THROUGH CONCEPTUAL UNDERSTANDING

As seekers come to a point in their Earth experience where it is obvious that what they are truly seeking is not available on the Earth, they must be able to see conceptually beyond the Earth. If their framework has been in the conceptual area, or to put it another way, if they have focused their Earth experience in a very rational, logical fashion, they must at this point begin to see logic beyond an Earth reference point.

For many, then, this is difficult. There is perhaps a holding point in their evolution until they can release the need to frame logic from the tangible or physical viewpoint. When this is released and they begin to conceptually frame-in existence in a holistic manner, then are they ready to see what IS truly.

Before that time, they have learned, they have grown, they have developed their physical abilities, many in great measure, many to the point of genius over the span of physical existence on the Earth.

Those that reach this point of evolution many times have been some of the leaders of your Earth. They have been great statesmen, great ballerinas, great musicians, great painters, priests who aided many. They have been writers who gave the Earth great works of literature. But, basically, what they have done is completed their evolution pretty much as far as Earth living is concerned. They may or may not be utilizing the conceptual abilities of self at the present time. But, even if they are, at this particular point, they must seek to approach existence and their understanding of it from a holistic or beyond the physical point of view.

Now those that have used their mental abilities extensively have an invaluable tool once they have made this major breakthrough. For many who have not perhaps viewed existence conceptually, these conceptual abilities must now be developed, expanded, and enhanced. Every ability is there in potentiality, so what we must do now is to look at how to begin to get in touch with conceptual abilities, what they are and why it is important to develop them. I say to you now, you are a part of the Oneness but to see it you have to be able to conceptualize the Oneness. That is the very basic goal. And thus I suggest a way to begin.

Let us consider the following: As a small child you have gone out to play and you are having a very good time but then you fall down and cut your knee on the sharp stones. Immediately, your attention focuses into the pain, does it not? Your play is forgotten, while you concentrate on the pain. You go running home to Mother, sobbing, and Mother takes you in her arms and says, "There, there, little one, it is all right. I will put a band aid on it and everything will be fine."

What has happened in this example? First, when you were playing and having a good time, you were enjoying existence, enjoying the learning experience. But after a specific point of trauma, of resistance, you focused in so much on the trauma that you were unable to again perceive the learning experience except through this point of trauma. You ran then to the one who symbolically represents the Source, your connection with it, your parent. Now, she told you with love and support that she would aid you and that everything would be all right. Thus you were able after that to skip back to your playmates and resume the learning experience, again seeing the pleasure of it.

What are we saying here? I am saying that by developing the concepts of the Whole, by seeing them, you stretch self beyond the point where you must focus on every little piece of resistance, every little painful episode on the Earth. You see how that specific which you are experiencing fits into the whole picture. By referencing always the whole plan, your life is focused here in physical existence on the purpose of evolution, the purpose of service within the Oneness, of evolving as the Oneness.

When you keep that conceptual umbrella over self, then although there may be some small traumas and a few that are not so small, you can look at self more objectively. You do not have to feel only pain and be totally unable to see beyond it. You can allow self to expand beyond that pain, and by working with it, remove the need ever to have it again. How? The conceptual abilities that have been developed show you that pain is something that you experience because of a misconception from your past. You do not have to retain it. You can choose to deal with specifics in that area of your misperceptions using a clearing system.

If you do not refer to the pain or trauma except as a misperception that you find interesting, although momentarily painful; if you can see your life in totality within the framework of the Source and Its learning, Its evolution; then, my friend, this will clarify your life and purposes. The Oneness is a personal reference for you (like the mother) because the Oneness is never impersonal. It is objective, but it cherishes, it nurtures, it supports each part of itself and you are one such part. You can ask the Source, your parent, to aid you when the going becomes painful and it will. It helps because when focused in your pain and asking for help from the Source, you objectify your experience. You begin to be cognizant of the conceptual framework under which you exist, your umbrella for existence, if you will.

Place an umbrella of your conceptual abilities over self. Know that this umbrella, this conceptual framework, is always there, and as you move forward in your evolution or on your path that we call your purposes, it moves with you. Thus it is necessary to understand, to conceptualize what you are in reference to the Oneness in an ever enlarging, more enhanced manner. The Source, Itself, has a conceptual outline for any particular Cosmic Day and as its evolution takes place, It also moves that conceptual outline forward. The Source's conceptual outline is the framework within which existence takes place. Without it, existence would be rather haphazard, unplanned, and not appropriately organized. When you can see that, then the ability to conceptualize will become one of your most important resources.

Now it is a very interesting exercise to take any concept and consider it. If you do this, several things happen. First you learn about that concept because you consider it from every point of view that you at that particular point can creatively bring forth. And as you fill in this conceptual outline, it becomes necessary because of evolution to move forward that conceptual outline which is the framework for your evolution. Therefore, by stretching self in an area, by conceptualizing through a specific focus, you evolve self and move forward your concept of what existence truly is.

Let me give you an example. We have talked about love being a lubricant by which all existence is smoothly run. If you can see that love is also a specific from which to conceptualize what existence is, that truly, when looking at existence through the eyes of love, every relationship within existence falls into the proper format. Love truly allows one to get rid of any sort of bias, any sort of prejudice, any sort of misconception or distortion that one may have about specifics in existence. Is it not wonderful that love mirrors for us the pieces of our existence? Love sorts out what you have perhaps misconstrued, and says, "Oh no." And when you look further in love, everything comes out exactly as it should. Love is the great equalizer, and of course I am talking about love in its highest, most conceptual sense.

To get in touch with love, one must be able to conceptualize what it is. For one thing, one must know that it is ever expanding because love is a part of the Source and evolution is a part of the Source. When we say it this way, you can see that looking at existence through love can be expanded every time you do so. That the first time you take it to what you think is the limit of your understanding, you will have framed existence through love and made a specific discovery. When you do it the next time, however, you should be able to go beyond that previous point to see love and its existence more and more real, to develop the relationships that shows you that love is real. But it is necessary first to frame the love unconditionally. It is the unconditional quality of the love that allows the full expression of what is real to be present.

Unconditional love is never especially sympathetic. Isn't that interesting? But in the fullest sense, sympathy means a feeling sorry for someone. Each person is Divinity. One does not feel sorry for Divinity. One may perhaps feel some compassion through love, through an attunement to the limitation that that divine spark has currently chosen to experience. But by conceptualizing what that divine spark is destined to be, then you see that sympathy is not appropriate.

Thus if you are compassionately focused in love, perhaps you seek to understand why some Earth beings are starving. Why is this being permitted? First, you must remember to conceptually align with the Oneness, refer to It beyond the Earth experience. You truly cannot understand a situation when you look at such a limited portion of it as the physical result. You must see the causal area of why this limitation has occurred. There are those in physical existence that have come into it rather recently. Many of them are in the developing countries. They do not yet see beyond what for them was a great trauma. For most, they were perhaps encouraged to come into physical existence, as many of you were also. But they have just begun. They are literally starving to death in their seeking to attune to anything. They have not yet seen the physical as a part of everything else. They accept a cut off state as their destiny.

Thus, physically, they cannot sustain their lives. What happens then? Some of these children of the light, because they are just that, get a glimmer of what is real. As many others come to the area seeking to aid them, they see the interactive, supportive quality that is beginning to stir in what is called the consciousness of humanity.

Look at the situation conceptually. What are we saying here? As those that are literally starving both physically and spiritually, seek to connect into the Oneness and have accepted a barrier here on the physical, humanity begins to respond to them. Why is that? Because, dear ones, Divinity is ever responsive to Divinity, when one accepts such help, such a support. As those who are starving expand their concept of what existence is, those that attune to them through unconditional love will respond, are responding to their physical needs. And of course, reflected beyond that is the response to their spiritual needs.

Now as these people come through this experience of near starvation and survive, there is a major breakthrough in their consciousness. Although the lesson continues that they have deemed necessary, it becomes eventually less and less severe until finally a break-even point in the consciousness is reached and the specific starving to death factor no longer is an prevalent as before. This is the way that evolution works. The mass consciousness of the group accepts an input from the beings within it. And if enough of them have specific misconceptions about anything, those misperceptions become very prevalent in the mass consciousness.

Thus each time there is a breakthrough by someone, it lightens this load, this limitation, this restriction within the mass consciousness. Those who experience a specific physical trauma will learn that this trauma is not encompassing. It is a specific focus within self that has accepted limitation. But if one conceptualizes beyond any such limitation to see that conceptual umbrella over which each of us exist, one can then see beyond, work beyond, this trauma.

Now it will be difficult for those newly in physical existence to have developed the conceptual abilities to see the Oneness from a physical standpoint. Evolution truly takes longer in sequential time than going from the beginning to the ending in just one or two lifetimes. Some of these developing nations must be allowed their experience. Certainly, if humanity through love wishes to aid them, I would say that is appropriate because they have invoked it by beginning to clear in that area. But recognize that mostly these peoples have only but begun their physical experiencing. Your New Age is not for them. They will be going to another physical experience to continue their learning.

The Source will learn also from those parts of Itself that are just beginning their physical existence now and will then have a slightly different vibrational pattern, a slightly different physical experience or planet in a few years. It is but another way to learn, one being of equal value to the other. And when you can conceptually see that evolution is framed from every point of view, then it truly is interesting to see what every point of view is.

That's my next point. If you are intellectually curious, and many of you are, then it is absolutely fascinating to see everything that is possible within the Source, within the evolutionary thrust. I am forever amazed. I am perhaps a little more experienced than most of you, and yet, I am constantly encountering new points of view as a Divine spark frames existence from a yet another point of view. Our Cosmic Day is now expanding at such a rapid rate that one could spend all of one's time or attention in seeing these refreshing approaches conceptually.

I am currently seeking to stretch beyond this Cosmic Day and see into the next one to consider how I would sound forth existence in the next one if I were the Source. (I don't mean to be presumptuous; it is an intellectual exercise only!) This exercise is stretching me forth conceptually, which is important because every point of view can be stretched by seeing beyond what currently is, not by enlarging a single focus, but by seeing the concept, the overall view of what is.

Conceptualizing is, in my opinion, attuning to the specific that you are within the Oneness, framing it into your current perception. Then, when you can conceive of your relationship with the Oneness, you constantly move it forward as you stretch your conceptual abilities. The best way to do it, as I said, is to analyze, to explore any specific subject fully and that will stretch your conceptual framework. I say to you, my friend, the conceptual ability to see what *is* will allow you to frame your existence, which is to serve as a focus that allows evolution to move forward. If you can see that, you can see why attuning to service and clearing out self will be the means to stretch self forward.

Service is the attunement to the purposes of the Cosmic Plan. That's what service is. You allow self to see that you are automatically evolving with the Source so you might as well cooperate. When you attune to this evolution, this path, this purpose, the way becomes much easier. It is the means by which you can joyously move forward. For some of you when focused into your lives with out seeing the Whole, without being able to conceptualize existence as it truly is, you cannot see that in spite of your non-clarity, evolution is taking place and you within it. Thus you can now see that you are a part of the Oneness that is evolving and your evolution will lead you forward.

The unconditional love for existence, for the Oneness, for the Wholeness, will lubricate that path of service and allow you to move forward. Can you see that love focus? This unconditional love, for the Source and its evolution, for all of existence, is the means to obtain what is real. And what is real is this service, this purpose, this path as everything evolves. Do not stumble on your path of evolution, do not resist it. Rejoice in the opportunity to serve. Do it unconditionally, knowing that self's evolution will be less traumatic, less painfully experienced when you do. Let go of the restrictions, let go of the limitations by conceptualizing the Oneness. See what existence is and join the multitude of those who have discovered the joy, the beauty of unconditional service.

CHAPTER 16

EXISTENCE AND ITS EXPANSIVE NATURE

I, perhaps more than any of you, view existence from a Wholeness perspective, a Oneness. But the physical focus is, truly, very special and gives one much opportunity to learn in the viewing process. Now, because of what you might call the "angle" from which one views Wholeness from the physical focus, the Wholeness often does not seem to be as present. One sometimes perceives a barrier. From a physical point of view, it is easy to do this - to perceive a barrier instead of the encompassing, all-pervading Wholeness or Oneness. This, truly, is an important key to opening up your perspective - to seeing beyond what you are focused upon now, physical existence. As you attempt, then, to align with Wholeness, to see that everything is right here where you are, to see beyond the physical barrier, do the following exercise. I think it will aid you a great deal. It is one that I did long ago as I approached the point where you are now. It was, for me, the key to going beyond this barrier that is truly not there at all, but is due to the reflected angle from which you view Wholeness, or my friends, seek to do so.

Sit in a chair, with your feet flat on the ground and your spine erect. Then visualize a large sheet of paper and see yourself at a specific point, represented by a dot. This is your physical focus. You are at the center of the creative process. Now, using that dot as a center point, draw a large circle around you. Now, what is in the center of that circle? It is you, but it is that Divine portion of you, your inner Divinity that is connected with every other part of the circle. You can see that by drawing a line now from where you are out to any point within the circle, you can connect with another focus. There could not possibly be any separation because everything, everyone connects. No matter which way you look, no matter which way you go, it all connects within the circle that we call Wholeness. It truly does not matter where you put your dot. Begin to move it around and experience that the dot still connects everywhere with Wholeness. However, when you begin to move it, you will find that your focus does not seem as balanced as it did in the center and being out of the center will require that you look differently at the Wholeness. Focused in the center is the best possible way from which to view Wholeness at the physical level.

Now, an additional exercise that will aid you is to use four of these horizontal circles or views of Wholeness. The first one we have already referenced. Then raise self up a level and focus in the center. Extend your circle again, remembering that you are connected with the one that you have already drawn. Do this four times until you have four points which are connected and four levels that rise, one above the other. This creates, then, a circle that is on four levels, each connected by the dot, or focus that interpenetrates through the center to the next level. This says that no matter what level you are on, in the sense of physical distance, you view Wholeness and will see it while focused on the physical plane because this plane interpenetrates the other levels. You can simply move your dot - move it to another level; go beyond the perspective of Wholeness on the physical. Now, this does not take away the physical focus which is the basis for your current stability. While you have that base, you can simply go above it, rise to the next level and the next and the next.

Now, the number of levels is truly limitless, but I have equated it to the four plane experiences - the physical, emotional, mental and spiritual - that are connected in the center by this dot. Truly, they all interpenetrate the same space. This is an exercise only to show you how your consciousness may journey into a different perspective while still focused here physically, while still based here on the physical plane. It is an exercise in expanding your perspective. If you think about it, the dot, which is representative of you, of your Divine focus, can be anywhere in existence. The dot is capable of being anywhere in all of the area, that is to say all of the state of being that the Creator - the Wholeness - has yet conceived. Each time the Wholeness opens up a new - what we might call "territory" - then you may journey there. The only thing that keeps you from traveling to any place right now is that you do not yet know it is possible when you are focused here on the physical level.

You have, then, four circles and they are one above another. Now, what would happen if you allowed the upper three circles to settle completely into and merge with the one that is on the physical level? Then we would still have the four circles, but they would truly interpenetrate one another. This is how Wholeness is put together: there are different levels of being that all interpenetrate into the same overall state of being. By taking the overall state of being apart a little and putting it together, we can see how the planes are constructed. You have come forth from this Wholeness. You are a point - a focus - within the Wholeness. When you understand the universal laws involved, you may view any point within this interpenetrating Wholeness that permeates everything.

Now, upon consideration this becomes an exercise in evolution. We have equated the Wholeness to the four planes that are interpenetrating one another. But if you go a step beyond that, you can see that existence is capable of sustaining as many of these interpenetrating circles as we can conceive of and more. Existence is not limited: it is ever expansive. You can keep adding your circles, keep interpenetrating the Whole with more levels forever. This is the way that existence expands. It is truly the way the Creator goes forth.

Each evolving consciousness participates actively in the experiencing of Divinity, of the Source. Now if we consider that statement, we can see that it leaves a wide range of perception as to what existence is and its mode of operation and evolvement. Each spiritual essence is an important part of Divinity and learns to function clearly in a balanced and real manner. Each Divine essence also looks at what is considered to be reality and decides for self what is real.

During an important part of the evolutionary path, one is very caught up in the illusion of the self. That is carefully phrased because all of us seek to understand that there truly is no one self, that the Self (with a capital S please) is Divinity, and any sort of a separateness is illusion.

When we consider self as separate, we form many illusions about existence and its purposes. This is very basic and is what each spiritual essence is seeking to understand. Truly self is Divinity. Djwhal Khul has stated many, many times that all that exists is Divinity and its experiencing. But let me now frame it a little differently, helping you to see that when you consider self at all as a separate unit, you are functioning within some illusion.

The amount of illusion depends upon the amount of separation with which you reference self. That is illusion, non-real. That is an image of self, this separateness that you experience. Most of you are seeking to understand that Divinity is a whole concept of which you are a part. Now, when you form conclusions that are clear and perceptive enough in the area of your relationship to Divinity as Divinity, you free yourself from physical existence.

There is a specific point at which you understand enough to release the illusion regarding physical existence. After this point, although you may experience physically if you choose, you do not have to and physical existence becomes real. It then contains no illusion. Another way of stating this is that human beings see an image of self only. They do not yet reference self in its "real" state.

To see the reality of self, one must begin to peel the layers of illusion. One must start to see Divinity as a complete focus for experiencing, to erase the separateness that for most exists as far as physical existence is concerned, to see clearly that self is Divinity expressing physically. As one truly realizes that the only real part of self is balanced, perceptive, divine - this becomes the way that physical existence is expressed.

The illusions of emotional trauma, imbalance and pain fall away when one realizes that the natural/the real state expressed physically is completely balanced, unrestricted, happy, conceptually active, service motivated, joyous, humble and group oriented. When one comes to these realizations, then one is approaching the point where physical existence is no longer "required." It becomes an optional course taken to train one as teacher.

This is a way of referencing what each of you are seeking to understand, to realize, that the only reality whether in physical existence or any other plane of existence is a stable, joyous state expressing true Divinity. Everything else is an illusion. We view life through an image, a pattern that we must erase, remove in order to see clearly, to realize completely what existence truly is.

When one reaches the point of functioning at soul level, a new beginning is activated. What are soul merged human beings seeking to understand? What have they yet to learn about self as Divinity? We have stated that to reach this point, you must see the real Self as Divinity. Is there yet more to realize, to recognize? Yes, there is.

Evolution is eternal. One is eternally making new realizations about Divinity. The soul-merged being seeks to understand that although he/she functions as a unit of Divinity, there truly is no such unit of Divinity, that the unit also is an illusion. Each must deal with this illusion and realize completely that it is one, that there truly exists nothing but the Source, and that everything that tends to be separate in the perceptions is an illusion. After understanding this completely, the soul-merged being then moves forward one more step on the ladder of evolution and begins looking at the next level of illusion that awaits in regard to understanding Divinity.

In my opinion, there will always be some illusion within self that we must sort out, we must dissolve. The Source Light Itself contains the means to expand and because this is built in to the creative process, we will always be dissolving the ending of our understanding and moving it to another level, a new beginning. This is another form of illusion. We believe sometimes at specific points in our evolution that we know everything, that there is nothing further to learn. This illusion is shattered by the realization that yet another learning experience must be assimilated into our understanding.

Each being reaches a point, usually several years after the soul-merge in sequential time, when Earth living - physical existence- -becomes optional.After this time, service becomes the only reference point for evolution. For some it is this total commitment to service that keeps them from permitting self to complete the Earth experience.

What I am saying is when you dedicate self unconditionally, this opens the door to your glorious future - to your complete unfoldment. I have stated this before in my teachings and I will continue to do so because it is such a crucial point. If there is any resistance to complete, unconditional service, know you are not yet ready to leave the Earth. That is one criteria, one way that you may evaluate your evolution. And, make no mistake, it must be unconditional.

Why is this? Because by giving us free will, the Creator knew that when we chose unconditional service, we could become aware enough, stable enough, understanding enough, strong enough within our Divinity pattern to complete the journey called physical existence   Unconditional service is the key that opens the door, it is the escape hatch, if you will, that leads from physical existence.

But one must not choose unconditional service to escape, because then it is not unconditional. Is it not interesting to see that the Source has realized exactly the needed pattern of awarenesses that each of us must realize in order to develop to the desired level, to come forth with joy, with gladness, with a caring, sharing attitude from the stint of experiencing in physical existence. Therefore, a specific criteria for the completing of our physical agenda is seeing clearly what unconditional service/dedication means and then making such a dedication. I encourage you to use a statement of unconditional dedication as an affirmation.

After physical existence your growth becomes easier or smoother. And why is that? It is because on the physical plane you must deal with resistance to aligning your will to the Cosmic will, to the Source's will. And once you have solved that completely, you are allowed to go beyond the physical level. This, truly, is the basis of what you are learning here in physical existence - to make that perfect alignment with the will aspect of the Source. The sooner you can allow self to perceive this, the more clearly you can plan how to get to this goal. It is your goal and I say to you now, "Recognize it and, by discipline within your life, work toward it."

You will also need to clear some of your blocks. Now, let's get into that a little. What are these blocks? These blocks are your misconceptions that have occurred on every level on which you have focused your experiencing. You must deal with them, understand them, move them out of the way so that you may perceive the will aspect of the Creator and align with it. That is what you are doing as you clear out your beliefs. Your clearness reflects back to the Source, Itself, what He is. You are a reflection of the Source and must learn to reflect It as clearly as It reflects into you. This is important to understand.

Look at it conceptually now. When all of you release misperceptions at your physical level, you become a lighter reflection for the Source. You allow this reflective quality (physical existence as you see it) to go out into existence. And it becomes the means to extend existence. It really goes forth and invokes further existence, It goes forth and allows existence to come into being. That is the key to the growth process of the Source, Itself. It is why you are working it out on the physical level. You are learning that by aligning your will with the Creator's and clearing out the blocks, you will truly reflect within self the Creator and His growing and His becoming that then goes forth and presents this opportunity to the Wholeness. This opportunity being presented is the means to go forward, the means to understand, to perceive, to learn, to evolve, to grow, to keep becoming. It is this means that is the key to all evolution. It truly is a privilege for all of us to have been individualized. It truly is a privilege to be allowed to come forth. It truly is a privilege that carries with it responsibilities. You are learning on the physical level what these responsibilities are. The time is coming when you say to self, "Yes, I am willing to serve in any capacity that will be helpful. If there is a need, I will respond." And so I say to you: "COME FORTH TO THE CALL OF YOUR SOUL."

You have invoked, through your desire to serve, many opportunities which will aid you. Each opportunity presents the means to, in a step by step process, make the realizations which can and will allow you to be free of having to remain within a physical structure.

It is important to see how going through a step by step realization process leads directly to freeing self from having to remain within a physical structure. For many of you as you serve now unconditionally, the realizations are coming rapidly and I am so glad, so supportive of each of you in your unfoldment. Remember, my friends, the true reality on the physical plane or any other plane is Divinity expressing harmoniously, joyously, caringly, and ever more encompassingly.

CHAPTER 17

THE CYCLE OF BEGINNINGS

We seek to understand the Oneness, Its perception, Its seekingness. In the beginning the Oneness contemplated, It reflected. As It did so, It began to experience. This was the beginning as far as we have understood it. You could see the Oneness as a ball. When It began Its experience, began to move toward greater understanding, then It began, in the sense of direction, to expand in every conceivable way.

But what about before such expansion began? Consider then the sphere. What was it before it was a sphere? We could equate it to a flat, two-dimensional circle, could we not? And before that, it was a one dimensional figure, a point. Do you see that although we equate the beginning to the Allness, that, of course, before the Allness, there were other beginnings on other levels, or, if you wish, in other states of perception that were also beginning? There is no beginning. There is only a change of perception that is ever growing, ever becoming.

Now, as you read these words, it becomes a little confusing to the finite mind. The mind looks for where to start. It looks for a beginning. But the beginning is simply a process of changing. And there has ever been changes within the Allness, the Oneness. If change is difficult for you, it is usually basically a difficulty of attunement to Oneness, to the constantly transforming Light.

How can you best understand that the Allness has ever been, has ever been transforming, has ever been evolving? Perhaps the best way to do so is to understand this: A specific concept is the result of many other concepts. It is formed as a conclusion from the analytical process. Therefore, the Oneness is a conclusion formed from several other conclusions that also are summaries of previous experiencing and, therefore, again conclusions. Now perhaps this is a good way to understand the Allness, that as It began to expand, as It began to evolve, It began to spiral forward. Existence grows and becomes in the spiral form. Now if you will consider this, there is a point at which we equate the beginning as we can perceive it. The journey of the Source Light began at this point in our understanding. However, It reached that point from another journey that we do not yet perceive.

The Source Light journeys in a large circle, a spiral. Now, to help you understand that all of existence was, is, and shall be at the same time, we will equate the journey of the Source Light to a Circle. The Source Light, then, a specific point on the circle. But that point is evolving, is growing, is changing. And as the journey continues, as the Source Light evolves, can you visualize, my friend, what happens to the Source Light? It becomes and grows and journeys in Its spiral. As it now goes forth in Its awareness, in Its becoming, in Its cycle of learning, who is to say that It does not again approach what It has been in this circle, in this cycle? Now It will approach it at a higher level in the spiral, you see. The circle becomes a spiral that is ever expanding. Thus Its awareness has increased as It approaches that specific point where It "began." But can you see also that each point within the circle is a new beginning? There are new beginnings at each point and that is how existence began. EXISTENCE BEGINS WITHIN THE ETERNAL NOW. Each point on the evolutionary spiral is a new beginning, is the beginning. There is no single beginning. Each point that is approached in awareness is a new beginning. This is how existence began. It always was beginning, It always has been. And to understand this, equate the circle to the spiral and equate that to a point that is ever becoming and has always been ever becoming.

Individualization comes about in a manner that is not discussed very often. It is the process of awakening within the Source, Itself, and as the Source awakens more and more fully, those potentialities within it come forth. Djwhal has said that sparks - individualized portions of the Creator - were created all at once, and that is true. But some are in the potential state only. As the Source stirs, as It learns, as It evolves, certain ones come forth at different interval periods. There is a great rhythm within the Allness and a beautiful rhythmic approach to growth and evolution.

Individualized sparks begin to experience at different focuses, or what would be called on the Earth different "times". This is not exactly accurate, of course, but one way of putting it into the eternal now connotation is to say that a specific focus becomes active at particular intervals. The active beginnings are the individualized portions of the Source Light. The Light individualizes as it focuses, as it creates an opportunity to understand more and more from these individualized points. You could say that the Source has not yet considered all of the unlimited potentialities of self, that it never will, that it keeps activating more of these potentialities. Each one of these potentialities is an individualized portion of itself that Djwhal has called "an evolving consciousness". His term is accurate enough even if rather limited. One must see beyond the individualized process and understand that an individual is but a focusing of the Allness. You could really equate this process to playing a beautiful instrument - perhaps a grand piano.

You produce sound as you stimulate or bring forth a certain combination of individual tones. The Creator, The Source, The Allness does this. He creates the music, the harmony of existence by stimulating or individualizing certain portions. Thus stimulated, they bring forth a specific poem of existence. Do you like that wording, "a poem of existence"? And there is a specific sequence to these poems. They are ever enlarging, ever becoming and each one is experienced and explored extensively. When the Source, the All-Knowingness, has created and completed this particular cycle that we have equated to a poem, It withdraws temporarily, digests and contemplates what It has experienced. This, too, is a cycle. When the Source, the Allness, has done this, has learned and digested from - and you could say "rested" from - the strenuous activity of the Cosmic Day, It goes forth again, cycles forth a new poem, a new combination of particular focuses, vibrations, and sounds that create yet another Cosmic poem. This is eternal, this happens continuously. In the sense of the Source Light, it is a specific rhythm that It has chosen to experience. The going forth during the Cosmic Day, the pulling in and contemplating during the Cosmic Night. It does not mean that there is destruction of anything during the Cosmic Night. It means that The Source becomes inactive, not experiencing in an active sense. The All-Knowingness, the Source, and Its specific focuses contemplate what has been experienced during the Cosmic Day.

Now, in the sense of sequential time, these Cosmic Days are very vast. It is not important right now to give you a sequential figure, but know they are much greater than heretofore given. Why is that? Because when one is focused in sequential time, it is almost impossible to understand from a perfectly balanced point of view what the Cosmic time clock actually is. Cosmic time is not time as you know it on the Earth. It is a stimulus of a focus, an activation process of a specific focus within the Source. The focus is there eternally. Sometimes it is active and sometimes it is not.

When first a specific focus is stimulated, is activated, we call this what Djwhal has said - the going forth process of the individual totality. Now, because the Source experiences everywhere and learns through every focus, It goes through the complete evolutionary spiral from every point. Every focus is a miniature replica of the Wholeness. We can see by discussing and learning about each miniature replica, what the Source, Itself, has gone through - how it has begun. If you contemplate that, it is awesome.

Do you believe - and this is just thrown out, now, for you to contemplate - that our Source, Itself, could be contained within yet a greater Source of which It is but a miniature replica? I ask this only as a question. I do not know the answer, but if there is no end to evolution and its evolvement, perhaps there is no end to its beginning. We might begin to consider that the proportions are only limited by our perceptions of them. Now, again this is meant but to whet your appetite for more; to seek to aid you to go within to contemplate the Source Light and your relationship to it. It is an exciting process, one that I continually do. One aspect of me, Vywamus, is always contemplating the Source Light and its evolution, knowing of course, that It is I and I am It, and there is absolutely no difference. But each time I do this, I find that *I learn a little. I find that I can go deeper.* There is no end, no beginning, only becoming, only growing, only evolving, only greater understanding and appreciation.

I wish now to take this a step further. To begin with, we have summarized the evolutionary process in terms of the Source Light and Its growth. And, of course, everything that exists is contained within this Source Light. The Source Light sends forth a

141

vibration, a specific combination of sound and each of you are a unique tone within the vibration that we call the Oneness. How, then, does your evolvement, your growth, fit into what I have said about the Oneness, about It's always having been there? It seems to me important to recognize that you are the Source from an individual perspective and that you seek to learn this, to understand, to perceive this absolute truth. People ask, "Is there absolute truth?" To me, the answer is "Yes." The absolute truth is the realization of your own individual perception of the Source Light. Now, your perception is never exactly the same as anyone else's. And it is not meant to be. We can learn together, but our perceptions will become a little refined and perhaps a bit reflective of our own uniqueness. As an individual perception of the Source Light, we have the ability to fit our perception within the Wholeness. This is magnificent when you can understand it thoroughly: it means that when you can find your individual niche in the overall Oneness, that you immediately attune to that Oneness, to that Wholeness. It is, therefore, the means to such an attunement. Now, as you approach the point where you begin to fulfill your purposes here on the Earth, and therefore within the Earth's Cosmic Plan, you begin more and more to find that special attunement with the Source Light. It becomes available to you through your spiritual channel. The means to open this spiritual channel is through finding, through locating your own unique perceptions, your own unique place in all of the Source Light. Now the purpose area that so many of you ask about, therefore, is the key to your evolution. As you begin to serve, to aid others, to fulfill these purposes, the alignment with the Source Light becomes more and more complete. This alignment involves becoming aware of your own harmony, of your own tone and then experiencing the vibration of the Wholeness through your own unique vibratory sound. The Oneness then reflects, harmonizes, reverberates through you. You can experience the Oneness as you approach your own unique path.

Now, this is exciting. The harmonics of your tone also aid you to approach the Source Light. Now, to me, Vywamus, this is the most harmonious, the most beautiful way to approach the Source: through your own vibration, contacting your own uniqueness deep within. This uniqueness being, remember, your own perception of the Source Light. This perception is not separate. It is but an individual part of the Source, a focus of the Source Light that contains perceptions. You are the Source. Can you see it? You are the Source. Can you feel it? You must be able to participate within your cosmic purposes as far as Earth living is concerned to begin to participate within the Source Light.

Now when you attune to the Source Light in this manner, the attunement is not traumatic. It is not difficult. It simply IS and the knowingness within self will respond to it. You literally become the harmonious embodiment of the Source Light. When you can function physically in this manner, completely, at least as far as your Earth experience is concerned, you will be approaching that goal of evolution that Djwhal has called the Third Initiation, AND, my friends, much beyond.

I, Vywamus, then, come to aid you to go beyond this point of evolution. Do not restrict yourselves to seeking the soul merge. Seek then the merging, the alignment with the Source Light. But do it in a specific way. Please understand the means by which you may harmoniously attune to the Source Light. For many of you here, now, this is the key to the next several steps in evolution for you. Of course, later in your evolution, you will understand more refined ways to do this same thing. But the process can be and should be started right here and now. Now consider it, then. Djwhal has emphasized that service is the key to your evolution and I agree with that. But, this is true because it makes you aware of your own unique perception of the Source Light and attunes you to it. This is the process that has begun as you now seek to fulfill those unique purposes.

Consider this, then. Your purposes may be from a specific perspective, but they are meant to exist and operate within the Oneness, within the Wholeness. If you still perceive a separation, feel that you are cut off from Oneness, this will interfere first in finding your unique purposes and second in attuning to the Oneness. I would suggest that the key for many of you is to work on self from the sense of feeling separate or cut off, or wanting to be visible or important within the cosmic plan for Earth.

One must truly understand that it is a blending of your efforts that leads you to perceive your own uniqueness. In a sense, when you go forth to serve the Cosmic Plan as many of you are beginning to do now, you pool your abilities into the Source Light again and you say, "Here they are. I dedicate self now to the Source. Use my abilities, use my energies. I come again. I do not qualify my dedication. I do not say I must be perceived in a specific way.

I give all to the Allness. I am ready to serve as I may. I am ready. Utilize me for such service where ever it is needed."

Now an interesting thing happens when you release the need to serve in a specific way. When you so release it, the higher aspect of self can begin to input to you its purposes in a very encompassing way. YOU GET WHAT YOU ARE SEEKING BY RELEASING THE NEED TO HAVE IT QUALIFIED. You see, it is important to perceive ways in which you can serve and utilize your strengths, but perhaps the Source Light or Its representatives can see those strengths more clearly than you. At the point where you make an unqualified dedication with all of the self, not just the intellectual part, but with the depths to which you can currently go or reach, then you open self to these potentialities. Then the Source Light knows that here is a worker, here is a server that may be utilized in the Oneness.

Now some of you have dedicated yourselves in this manner and you sit and you wait. And you wait.

And you wait and nothing seems to be happening. And you say,"But I have dedicated self. I have said "I will serve, now use me." You wait and your physical existence becomes restricted, becomes limited. Nothing seems to be happening. What is the problem? Why has not this service begun?

Well my friends, it has begun on the higher levels, on the spiritual plane, but it has not yet begun on the Earth plane. And why not on the Earth plane yet? Why has not everything suddenly fallen into place? Well, perhaps one must consider the nature of Divinity Itself to understand that.

Divinity creates. Divinity is the creative process that goes forth and experiences and learns and becomes and shares and is. You are Divinity. You are focused here on the Earth. All that you have to do after making such a dedication is to go forth as Divinity and begin to serve. This is your physical responsibility and you learn by doing so. It was never meant for the spiritual realm to do the creating for you on the physical realm. This is a focus into physical existence which you are currently experiencing that gives you an opportunity which is unique. Now, this does not mean that you may not have, in fact you will develop, perfect attunement to the Source Light when you have opened it through purposefully creating your own uniqueness within the Creator's Cosmic Plan here on the Earth plane.

Do you see that YOU have the responsibility to create what you have dedicated to do? You have made a dedication and thus agreed to serve unqualifyingly. Take that responsibility. Go forth on the Earth plane and create it. Again, perfect attunement can aid you. The Source Light and the Divinity that you perceive as your own uniqueness will support you. That truly is all of the support that you could ever need, want or desire. Separated as you were before, you perceived your own wants, needs, and desires as being important. Now see after you dedicate yourself completely where you really place those wants, needs and desires within the Source Light, and know that they will be met, they will be supported by your own Divinity and the attunement to the Source Light.

WHAT THIS ALL MEANS IS THAT YOU MUST NOW GO FORTH ON THE EARTH PLANE AND JOYFULLY CREATE YOUR PART OF THE CREATOR'S COSMIC PLAN FOR EARTH. Now remember, I did not say to serve "separately." I said to find your own unique part within the Oneness. So seek to understand that you are Divinity that creates for the Source Light. This is your purpose on the Earth. You are not to be passive about the creative process. You are to align your will within the Creator's Plan and purposefully move forward with the Light. We evolve together. We are the Source. We are the Oneness.

I can hear some of you saying, "But I do not know my purposes. I do not know what to do." After making such a dedication, the first step is to recognize that you have done it. Now that may sound strange but it is not. It means that once this dedication is realized completely, everything becomes dif-

147

ferent. There is an instant inner attunement to the Source Light as never before. You are not the same. Your perception has turned a 90 degree angle. You have become the means by which the Creator may move forward. You have removed the separateness perception, at least on the inner plane.

You must now do what? Erase the *effects* of the separateness that have been present up to this point on the outer planes. Now, this is probably the most important thing I've said so far. On the outer planes you will still experience, for a while, the effects that you created before you became dedicated 100% to serve the Source Light. You can choose to deal with these effects and move them into more complete harmony with your new purposes.

Now, I am not saying that if you have current responsibilities, you must push them aside and say, "I am not going to do that anymore." Of course not. But by going within, by seeing how these responsibilities fit within this glorious Cosmic Plan, you really will be able to move your life into the service vehicle more and more completely.

There must be a complete release of what has been. For many of you this is symbolic. For others it is actual. It means then that you must be willing to release your Earth experience as it has been in the past. Many times, just by being willing to release it completely, you do not have to do so. If your service takes you into other areas where you need to be completely free, you may have to release everything. The point is you must be willing to do so. This, again, does not mean and do not take it to mean that I am telling you to run away from your current responsibilities. Commitments that have been made must be fulfilled or realigned or reunderstood. You have to deal with yourself right where you are now.

The point is that you can do it. You will do it because you have become a Source vehicle. Think about that statement. You have become a Source vehicle that is serving on the physical plane. You will be here on the physical plane serving the Source Light in totality. I want you to understand that that is what begins when you make such an unqualified dedication.

Again, let me also emphasize that you must create such a Source vehicle. You must deal with whatever effects are there that you have also created. You must purposefully move forward as a server, dealing with whatever needs to be handled or dealt with. You must see that this ever increasing attunement to the Source Light can support you and sustain you. Far from being cut off from anything, by your dedication you begin to perceive more and more support from the Source Light. Now if you consider that statement, you can realize that you have never been cut off. But your perception up to that point for many of you is that you have been. Earth living is perceived from a separateness point of view by many.

Mankind has opportunities now that can be seen much more clearly from the spiritual plane. Now spiritual existence is much greater, much more encompassing than is considered possible in physical existence. As one unfolds, as one develops on the spiritual plane, one begins to glimpse all levels of existence. You become acquainted with the multiplicity of existence that does resolve into Oneness, but you see it through a layered effect. The structure of existence becomes what one might call crystal clear. You are able to focus on a specific level, as all of you are doing now by focusing on the physical level. But in your spiritual development, you begin to see the layered, the many focused totality. This means that you become much enriched by viewing different focuses of experiencing.

The Source Light, as I have stated earlier, sounds forth a specific poem of creation for a specific Cosmic Day. It becomes an intermingling of sound, of vibration, that creates this opportunity for experiencing, for learning, for evolving, for growing. How does this particular Cosmic Day begin? What choices are made? How is it decided what will be sounded forth? How does the creative process start? Have you considered it?

We consider it miraculous, much beyond comprehension, until we begin to view in our spiritual existence, in our spiritual totality truly, the multiple layers. The way each layer relates to every other layer. We begin to sense the unfoldment, the drama of experiencing, of learning, of becoming. Each layer, in a sense, leads forth the next or unfolding layer. It is rather easy when viewed from your totality to what? To predict what will follow in the unfoldment of the next level.

Now when you have reached a specific point of unfoldment, evolvement, you begin to see also the next level and its probable and potential unfoldment. You begin to see how each level relates to each of the others in its complete potentiality. Then truly can you begin to see the interrelationship between one Cosmic Day and the next. You see, the Days unfold also. We exist in a specific Cosmic Day. If we could glance at what the last Cosmic Day contained, we could see what is unfolding in this one and what will probably unfold in the next. We can see the trends; let me tell you about our Cosmic Day. The Cosmic Day we are focused in right now is not a young one. Cosmic Days are a vast concept and the present one is only one of perhaps one million that have already transpired. Now, that is a generalization, there, a rounding out of figures. I am not stating it exactly.

What is coming? Well, you could say these Cosmic Days are eternal, never ending, unfolding and always going forth. We are somewhere within sequence of Cosmic Days with the potential being unlimited and never ending. Now if you consider that, what could possibly be true about this Cosmic Day that hasn't been true about the other ones that have already transpired that add up to be almost a million? Each Cosmic Day is a unique interpretation of existence. If we look back to the first few, we find first of all that they were not as complex. There weren't as many levels and there was not as much richness to the unfoldment of existence.

The Source Light has enriched itself many, many fold as it has developed, grown, understood, and contemplated each Day. You see, it is no accident that the spiritual teachers say to you, "Reflect upon your day as it is ending. Consider what you have learned. Consider what has gone on." This is a good way to learn about self. The Source Light does this with great comprehension at the end of each Cosmic Day, reflecting, studying, learning. Thus, when it composes, when it writes the next Day, It embellishes and enriches it. The new day is more comprehensive.

Does this not say that because we have had perhaps a million Cosmic Days before this one, existence has been enriched, embellished, added to, and comprehended much more fully than many of us, including myself, can see at this point? I have learned that when in physical existence, if you engage in an activity that reflects the activity of the Source Light Itself, then there is a direct attunement to the Source Light. Thus, when you contemplate, reflect on your own day, then you move up the layers of self awareness, of your consciousness, until you connect with the Source Light and Its reflection or contemplation.

Now you may say to me, "But this Cosmic Day is still going on. There is not yet a contemplative period by the Source Light. If there were, we would not be still experiencing." And I say, "That is true." But remember, in the non-sequential time, one may connect with anything that exists. You simply have to focus it, because that is what time is on the spiritual plane - a focus. When you reflect, ponder your day, focus into the Cosmic pondering, the Cosmic reflection, then you can truly connect with this beautiful, enlarged, encompassing contemplation.

What will you gain by this? You, for one thing. move your contemplation to a level of complete free-flowingness. If the conceptual area of self is very open, you begin to enlarge the concepts by stretching into what has been referred to as the Universal Mind. You begin to receive many concepts that are directly connected with the reflection, with the contemplation of the Source. in a whole totality of such contemplation.

Now we could talk about this for days. I have thought about it. I utilize this technique extensively. In fact, to get personal about it, I feel this technique has aided me more than any one thing that I currently do - the ability to attune to the Source Light's contemplation and reflection, and thus, gain from its experiencing. You see, we are a part of the totality, the Source Light, and we can benefit by its learning experience. This is a suggestion for those of you that can see what it offers and will make the effort to work with it.

If you experience difficulty in attuning to the Source Light's contemplation the first time, keep trying. Probably the way that you can validate it is when the specific ideas and specific understandings from receiving such ideas really begin to tumble over one another. Then know that you really have opened your channel TO THE SOURCE LIGHT IN ITS CONTEMPLATIVE FOCUS. Isn't that an interesting statement! Am I saying, here, that we may open our channel to specific focuses besides individuals, besides our own soul? I certainly am!

You may connect in very specific ways into the Source Light and its VARIOUS modes of experiencing. What are you seeking to learn? Can you utilize this technique? I say to you, "Yes, you can when you know how to do so." It is the natural teacher that we are referencing here. What do I mean by that? Divinity - the totality of Divinity - is experiencing and because it is a very experienced totality of Divinity, we can learn from it. It is the ultimate teacher for each of us when we can utilize the channeling techniques that we are learning, that you are getting from the spiritual teachers, including me, when you can utilize them to channel what has been learned into self. This is a goal and we will do it together.

Now many times we cannot see the "size" of Creation. It doesn't matter anyway because as you grow, as you learn, as you unfold, you begin to glimpse that it is much greater than you previously understood. This expansion of your understanding is a constantly unfolding process. When you can glimpse the next level, you see that it is much greater than the previous level, much greater than you had considered. You reach the next level of understanding and the same thing happens again. You are always getting a glimpse, truly, that Creation is much greater than you have formerly seen.

I am sure that I, Vywamus, have had only a glimpse of what truly exists in this area of the creative part of the Source Light. I am beginning, only beginning, to sense Its true potentialities. But I have recently come to an important conclusion that I feel is valid. Again, I may be just getting a glimpse of what I have begun to sense, but I do believe that I am correct. I have been sensing that the Source Light is expanding at a rate which is truly awesome. But its expansion has now begun to change. For the first time in all of existence, in all of its experiencing as a Wholeness, on Its level of origination that we call the Source Light, It is changing in a direction, in a multiplicity of exchange of the molecules, if you will, but not in a physical sense. The molecules of the creative force are expanding, are literally exploding as never before.

Now, how shall I put that? Well, the creative force, the vibration, the sounding forth, has been going for approximately one million Cosmic Days. Now this Cosmic Day is about three-quarters completed. After the completion of this Cosmic Day there will come a new type of Cosmic Day. We, being a part of the Source Light, will see existence in a more complex, more multi-dimensional, multi-layered way than ever before. There will be a new mode of existence developed and this is starting right now.

You see, the ever expanding, ever changing Source Light is always looking for a new way, a new level, a new inner penetration to explore. Such a way is being developed right now. Now it is not a part of this Cosmic Day, but remember, it is coming soon in

155

the sense of Cosmic Time and one can begin to attune to it. I have done so. That is why I tell you I am sensing a great event within the Source Light, Itself.

This says something very important and that is why I am referring to it. The Source Light has connected with a great potentiality of self, a change that will enrich it, that will enable it to understand in a different way, in a different focus, enlarging its experiencing and its comprehension of experiencing, of moving forth, of evolving. So what does this mean? It means that when you plug into the Source Light's unfoldment, when you can plug into its reaching for its potentialities in a rather concrete way, spiritually speaking, you can get in touch with your own potentialities in a more concrete, physically manifesting way. It is why I am going into it. You can learn to plug into these potentialities.

In a specific sense, what you will be plugging into is free-flowingness, but a specific focus of it. So we have invited a being named Alazaro, who has recently come to the earth to aid the Earth to plug into free-flowingness in as many ways as she can currently conceive of. She is a specialist in all creation in free-flowingness and has seen it in more ways than I can give you here.

If you will get in touch with her personally through your own channel, she can help you to plug into the Source Light in Its unfoldment of Its potentialities at this particular Cosmic time and aid you to do the same thing in your own individual reflection of the Source Light. You can learn to utilize the Source

Light and Its understanding in Its unfoldment in a reflected way. In the New Age, she will be coming to the Earth within a physical structure of her own. But right now she is available through attunement through your own channel and through teachings that are presented.

Alazaro is what we call a "transfer" from the angelic kingdom, who is coming now into the unfoldment, the evolvement of self that she has earned. Now that does not mean that the angelic kingdom is any less, than the evolving consciousness. It simply means it is different, for different purposes. Alazaro now is needed here on the Earth and so because of her dedication, she has changed her application of divinity. That is what it means.

Alazaro will aid you to reach the free flow level that will help you to utilize the Source Light's growth. And I say to you, "Pay attention! Take advantage of this opportunity." Now, you may also try it yourself. Please do. In a state of meditation, see the Source Light reflecting, see Its learning and going into specifics beyond which you understand now but just know that It has reached a critical point of understanding Utilize your own free-flowingness together with the Source Light's free-flowingness to learn, to comprehend what is transpiring here and now.